INSTANT COMMUNICATIONS

— Whether you are encountering Russians in their homeland or hosting them here

— Whether you are facing a restaurant menu or a hotel desk clerk

— Whether you are visiting a museum or stopping at a gas station

— Whether you need directions or want to strike up a casual conversation

— Whether you have to deal with a medical emergency or a mechanical breakdown

— Whether you want to establish trust and good feelings in a business meeting or demonstrate warmth and courtesy in personal dealings

This one book is your

PASSPORT TO RUSSIAN

PASSPORT TO
RUSSIAN

Charles Berlitz

WITH THE COLLABORATION OF
Marina Igorevna Petrova

A SIGNET BOOK

SIGNET
Published by New American Library, a division of
Penguin Group (USA) Inc., 375 Hudson Street,
New York, New York 10014, USA
Penguin Group (Canada), 90 Eglinton Avenue East, Suite 700, Toronto,
Ontario M4P 2Y3, Canada (a division of Pearson Penguin Canada Inc.)
Penguin Books Ltd., 80 Strand, London WC2R 0RL, England
Penguin Ireland, 25 St. Stephen's Green, Dublin 2,
Ireland (a division of Penguin Books Ltd.)
Penguin Group (Australia), 250 Camberwell Road, Camberwell, Victoria 3124,
Australia (a division of Pearson Australia Group Pty. Ltd.)
Penguin Books India Pvt. Ltd., 11 Community Centre, Panchsheel Park,
New Delhi - 110 017, India
Penguin Group (NZ), 67 Apollo Drive, Rosedale, North Shore 0745,
Auckland, New Zealand (a division of Pearson New Zealand Ltd.)
Penguin Books (South Africa) (Pty.) Ltd., 24 Sturdee Avenue,
Rosebank, Johannesburg 2196, South Africa

Penguin Books Ltd., Registered Offices:
80 Strand, London WC2R 0RL, England

Published by Signet, an imprint of New American Library,
a division of Penguin Group (USA) Inc.

First Signet Printing, September 1992
20 19 18 17 16

Contents

Preface

Is it possible to learn to speak Russian from a phrase book? If one means basic communication—the ability to speak, understand, and generally get along—the answer is yes, *if* you learn the right phrases. The secret of learning languages is to learn not only individual words but the phrases in which they are apt to occur with frequency, as native Russians use them every day.

The concept of this book is to provide instant communication in Russian. The phrases are short, geared to situations of daily life, and pinpointed for easy reference so that you can find the exact section you need at any moment.

There is even a chapter—"Words That Show You Are 'With It'"—which gives you the key words and phrases that Russian people use to add color to their conversation. In this way, instead of learning about "the umbrella of my aunt," you learn to use the right phrase at the right time, in the very way a Russian person would use it. And, so that the person you are addressing will understand your accent, all you have to do is read the phonetic line under each Russian phrase *as if it were English.*

Further practice and listening to Russian people speak will help you constantly improve your accent.

The use of this book is not limited to a trip to the U.S.S.R. Russian is an increasingly important world language, and in addition to the pleasure and help you will get by speaking Russian on your travels, you will enjoy using the idiomatic Russian phrases in this book in Russian restaurants or stores at home and with Russian-speaking people you may meet anywhere.

A section about business affairs is also included, now especially appropriate because of the Soviet Union's increasing importance in international trade. Use of this business vocabulary will facilitate your dealings with Russian business contacts, another advantage "glasnost" and "perestroika" have created between Russia and the West.

Travelers using phrase books sometimes complain that when they ask a question or make a request to a native speaker of the language they cannot understand the answer they get. This has been solved in *Passport to Russian* by an original and effective expedient. After the first few sections a special insert called "Point to the Answer" appears at the end of various sections. You simply show this section, which requests the person to whom you are speaking in Russian to point to the appropriate answer. This is an assured way of instant and exact communication, and besides its evident usefulness, it will give added confidence. Since you are communicating in this way with a Russian-speaking person, it also will constantly improve your understanding of the language.

Students studying Russian in a more conventional manner in school or college will find this book an invaluable aid to their studies in that it brings modern colloquial Russian alive as a means of communication.

The use of this book will more than double your enjoyment of a trip abroad and also help you save money. Besides the economic factor, why visit a foreign country if you can't break the language barrier and communicate with the new and interesting people you meet? You might as well stay home and see the palaces and monuments of the country on color TV. Who wants to be limited to one language when picking up another language can be so easy and enjoyable?

One can speak and understand current everyday Russian with comparatively few words and phrases—perhaps 1,600 to 1,900, which is less than the number given in the special dictionary at the end of this book. By using the same short constructions over and over, in the various situations where they normally occur, you will acquire them without conscious effort. They will become a part of your own vocabulary and of your memory bank, and that is, after all, the only secret of learning a language.

How to Perfect Your Russian Accent and Learn the Russian Letters

The phrases in *Passport to Russian* are written in English, Russian, and easy-to-use English phonetics. Read the third line as if it were English, stressing the syllables written in capital letters. This stress is important in order for Russians to understand you when you speak to them. Until you learn the Russian letters use the third line for immediate communication. You can also *show* the book to a Russian, pointing to the second line that translates exactly what you wish to say.

As you progress in spoken Russian try to identify the Russian printing (second line) with the phonetic pronunciation of the third line. The following *sound values* of the letters in the Russian (or Cyrillic) alphabet will help you to recognize easy words and eventually to understand and pronounce them. The letters below are arranged in the Russian alphabetical order.

RUSSIAN LETTER	ENGLISH APPROXIMATE SOUND USED WITHIN A WORD
А	ah
Б or б	b
В	v (pronounced "f" when ending a word)
Г	g (pronounced "k" when ending a word)
Д	d (pronounced "t" when ending a word)
Е	yeh or eh
Ё	yo
Ж	zh
З	z
И	ee
Й	like y in "boy" or "you"
К	k
Л	l
М	m
Н	n
О	o (or *ah* when its syllable is *unstressed*)
П	p
Р	r
С	s
Т	t
У	u
Ф	f
Х	kh (guttural, as in the Scottish "loch")
Ц	ts
Ч	ch
Ш	sh
Щ	sh'ch
Ъ	(hard sign)
Ы	(open I as in "bit" and "bird")
Ь	(a "soft" sign, softening the preceding consonant)
Э	eh
Ю	yoo
Я	ya

The Cyrillic alphabet has 33 letters, including two "silent" ones, the Ъ or "hard sign", which separates the hard, final sound of a prefix from an initial, soft vowel (preceded by the sound "yeh") and the Ь or "soft sign" which softens the preceding letter. As you read each section compare the phonetic line with the Russian lettered second line. You will see that most of the letters correspond with English letters or English letter combination. There are, however, two exceptions, the Ж has the sound of "s" in pleasure or treasure; we have written it phonetically as "zh." And the Russian X is like a guttural English "h" which we express in the phonetics as "kh". In addition, the *unaccented* "o" is pronounced like a broad "a" (ah), and the Г, Д and В (in English, the "g," "d," and "v") are pronounced as "k," "t," and "p," when used as a *final* letter. The *names* for each Russian letter can be found in the "Telephone" section (page 104) where you will need them for spelling names, etc. But the way they sound will help you to recognize and memorize the Russian words in the second line of each sentence.

Once you begin to recognize and memorize the Russian letters you should try to decipher signs and posters you may see written in Russian as well as place names and street signs, names of stores, advertisements, and such. This will make any walk you take around a Russian city not only a diversion but also, as my grandfather, Maximilian Berlitz (who operated a number of his language schools in Russia) used to tell me, this will provide an extra and constant language practice during your travels in this colorful and historic country.

PASSPORT TO
RUSSIAN

1. Greetings and Introductions

Greetings! (Good health!) (Can be used at any time of day.)
Здравствуйте!
ZDRAHST-vwee-t'yeh!

Good morning.
Доброе утро.
DOH-bra-yeh OO-tra.

Good day.
Добрый день.
DOH-bree d'yen'

Good evening.
Добрый вечер.
DOH-bree V'YEH-cher.

How are you?
Как вы поживаете?
kahk vwee pa-zhee-VA-yeh-t'yeh?

Fine, thanks, and you?
Хорошо, спасибо, а вы?
ha-ra-SHO, spa-SEE-ba, ah vwee?

Come in, please.
Войдите, пожалуйста.
voy-DEET-yeh, pa-ZHAHL'-sta.

Sit here, please.
Садитесь здесь, пожалуйста.
sa-DEET-yes zd'yes', pa-ZHAHL'-sta.

May I introduce...
Можно вам представить...
MO-zhna vahm prehd-STA-veet'...

Very happy (to meet you). (Spoken by a man)
Очень рад.
OH-chen' raht.

Very happy (to meet you). (Spoken by a woman)
Очень рада.
OH-chen' RA-da

My name is...
Меня зовут...
meh-N'YA za-VOOT...

Your name?
Ваше имя?
VA-sheh EEM-ya?

Where are you from?
Откуда вы?
aht-KOO-da vwee?

I am from Moscow.
Я из Москвы.
ya eez mahsk-VWEE.

And you?
А вы?
ah vwee?

I am American. (mas.)
Я американец.
ya ah-meh-ree-KA-n'yets.

I am American. (fem.)
Я американка.
ya ah-meh-ree-KAHN-ka.

Welcome to Russia!
Добро пожаловать в Россию!
dahb-RO pa-ZHA-la-vaht' v' ra-SEE-yoo!

Thank you very much.
Большое спасибо.
bahl-SHOY-yeh spa-SEE-ba.

You are very kind.
Вы очень добры.
vwee OH-chen' dahb-REE.

Good-bye.
До свидания.
da svee-DAHN-ya.

Good night.
Спокойной ночи.
spa-KOY-nay NO-chee.

Note: Russian does not use an equivalent word for Mr., Mrs., or Miss, but employs the word "Citizen" — *гражданин* (grahzh-da-NEEN) for males and *гражданка* (grahzh-DAHN-ka) for females. This title is used on governmental or formal occasions. For foreigners the word *господин* (ga-spa-DEEN) (male) or *госпожа* (ga-spa-ZHA) (female) is used, a relic of former days, literally "master" or "mistress." Today one normally uses a person's first and middle (patronymic) name together or, upon better acquaintance, just the first name. See also page 124.

2. Basic Expressions

Learn these by heart. You will use them every time you speak Russian. If you memorize the expressions and the numbers in the next section, you will find that you can ask prices or directions and generally make your wishes known.

Yes.
Да.
da.

No.
Нет.
n'yet.

Perhaps.
Может быть.
MO-zhet bweet'.

Of course.
Конечно.
kahn-YETCH-na.

Please.
Пожалуйста.
pa-ZHAHL'sta (or) pa-ZHA-lis-ta (usually said as with the first example).

Thank you.
Спасибо.
spa-SEE-ba.

You are welcome.
Не за что.
N'YEH za ch'ta.

Excuse me (or) I'm sorry.	**It's all right.**
Извините.	Это хорошо.
eez-vee-NEE-t'yeh.	*EH-ta ha-ra-SHO.*

Note: One should always use пожалуйста (*pa-ZHAHL'-sta*), meaning "please" when asking questions or making requests. It can also function for "Bring me...," "I want...," or "I would like...," followed by the word for whatever you need.

"It's nothing," "You are welcome," or "It doesn't matter" can all be expressed by ничего (*nee-cheh-VO*), which means "nothing."

When you ask a question or start a conversation with a stranger, it is useful to begin with "Excuse me, please." Извините (*eez-vee-NEE-t'yeh, pa-ZHAHL'-sta*) without adding "sir" or "madame" as you might in English.

How much?	**This.**	**That.**
Сколько?	Это.	Тот.
SKOHL'-ka?	*EH-ta.*	*toht.*

Where?	**Here.**	**There.**
Где?	Здесь.	Там.
gd'yeh?	*zd'yes'.*	*tahm.*

Who?	I	you	he	she	it	we	they
Кто?	Я	вы	он	она	это	мы	они
k'toh?	*ya*	*vwee*	*ohn*	*ah-NA*	*EH-toh*	*mwee*	*ah-NEE*

Is it far?	**How much time?**
Это далеко?	Сколько время?
EH-ta da-leh-KO?	*SKOHL'-ka v'REM-ya?*

How much money?
Сколько денег?
SKOHL'-ka D'YEH-nek?

How?	**Like this.**	**Not like this.**
Как?	Так.	Не так.
kahk?	*tahk.*	*n'yeh TAHK.*

It is possible.	**Not possible.**
Возможно.	Не возможно.
vahz-MOHZH-na.	*n'yeh vahz-MOHZH-na.*

When?	**Now.**	**Not now.**
Когда?	Сейчас.	Не сейчас.
kahg-DA?	*seh-CHAHSS.*	*n'yeh seh-CHAHSS.*

Later.	**Soon.**
Позже.	Скоро.
PO-zheh.	*SKO-ra.*

That is very good.	**...very bad.**	**Really?**
Это очень хорошо.	...очень плохо.	Верно?
EH-tah OH-chen' ha-ra-SHO.	*...OH-chen' PLO-ha.*	*VEHR-na?*

It's important.	**It doesn't matter.**
Это важно.	Ничего.
EH-ta VAHZH-na.	*nee-cheh-VO.*

3. Numbers

1
один
ah-DEEN

2
два
dva

3
три
tree

4
четыре
cheh-TEE-reh

5
пять
p'yaht'

6
шесть
shest'

7
семь
s'yem'

8
восемь
VO-s'yem'

9
девять
D'YEHV-yaht'

10
десять
D'YEHS-yaht'

11
одиннадцать
ah-DEE-naht-tsaht'

12
двенадцать
d'veh-NAHT-tsaht'

13
тринадцать
tree-NAHT- tsaht'

14
четырнадцать
cheh-TEER-naht-tsaht'

15
пятнадцать
p'yaht-NAHT-tsaht'

16
шестнадцать
shest-NAHT-tsaht'

17
семнадцать
s'yem-NAHT-tsaht'

18
восемнадцать
vo-sehm-NAHT-tsaht'

19
девятнадцать
dehv-yaht-NAHT-tsaht'

20
двадцать
DVAHT-tsaht'

21
двадцать один
DVAHT-tsaht' ah-DEEN

22
двадцать два
DVAHT-tsaht' dva

23
двадцать три
DVAHT-tsaht' tree

24
двадцать четыре
DVAHT-tsaht' cheh-TEE-reh

25
двадцать пять
DVAHT-tsaht' p'yaht'

30
тридцать
TREED-tsaht'

40
сорок
SO-rahk

50
пятьдесят
p'yaht-d'yeh-s'YAHT

60
шестьдесят
shest-d'yeh-s'YAHT

70
семьдесять
s'yem-d'yeh-s'YAHT

80
восемьдесят
vo-s'yem'-d'yeh--s'YAHT

90
девяносто
d'yev-ya-NO-sta

100
сто
sto

200
двести
dv'YEH-stee

300
триста
TREE-sta

400
четыреста
cheh-TEE-r'yeh-sta

500
пятьсот
p'yaht-SOHT

600
шестьсот
shest-SOHT

700
семьсот
s'yem-SOHT

800
восемьсот
vo-s'yem-SOHT

900
девятьсот
d'yev-yaht-SOHT

1000
тысяча
TEE-s'ya-cha

2000	**3000**	**100,000**
две тысячи	три тысячи	сто тысяч
dveh	*tree-TEE-*	*sto TEE-say'ch*
TEE-s'ya-chee	*s'ya-chee*	

1,000,000	**1st**	**2nd**	**3rd**
миллион	первый	второй	третий
meel-YOHN	*P'YER-vwee*	*fta-ROY*	*TR'YEH-tee*

last	**half**	**zero**
последний	половина	ноль
pa-SLED-nee	*pa-la-VEE-na*	*nohl*

How much? (or) How many?	**What number?**
Сколько?	Какой номер?
SKOHL'-ka?	*ka-KOY NO-mer?*

4. Arrival

Besides talking with airport officials, one of the most important things you will want to do on arrival in Russia is to find your way around. In this section you will find some basic "asking your way" questions and answers. We call your attention to the "Point to the Answer" sections, at the end of some lessons, which Russians can use to point out answers to make it easier for you to understand.

Your passport, please.
Ваш паспорт,
   пожалуйста.
vahsh PA-sport,
   pa-ZHAHL-sta.

I'm a tourist.
Я турист.
ya too-REEST.

I'm on a business trip.
Я в командировке.
ya v' ka-mahn-dee-ROHF-
   keh.

...several weeks.
...несколько недель.
...N'YEH-skohl'ka
   n'yeh-D'YEL'.

Where is the baggage?
Где багаж?
gd'yeh ba-GAHZH?

from flight forty.
с рейса 40.
s' RAY-sa SO-rahk.

This is my baggage.
Это мой богаж.
EH-ta moy ba-GAHZH.

Where is the Customs?
Где таможня?
gd'yeh ta-MOHZH-n'ya?

This is mine.
Это моё.
EH-ta ma-YO.

(Shall I) open it?
Открыть?
aht-KREET'?

Yes. Open, please.
Да. Откройте, пожа-
  луйста.
*da. aht-KROY-t'yeh,
  pa-ZHAHL'-sta.*

**I have nothing to de-
  clare.**
Я меня нечего объяв-
  лять.
*oo meen-YA neh-cheh-VO
  ahb-yev-L'YAHT'.*

Wait!
Подождите!
pa-dazh-DEE-t'yeh!

A suitcase is missing.
Потерялся чемодан.
*pa-teh-r'YAL-sa
  cheh-ma-DAHN.*

Where do I report it?
Где об этом заявить?
*GD'YEH ab EHTOM zah-
  yah-VEET'?*

Is this yours?
Это ваше?
EH-ta VA-sheh?

Yes, it's mine.
Да, это моё.
da, EH-ta ma-YO.

Many thanks.
Большое спасибо.
*bahl'-SHOH-yeh
  spa-SEE-ba.*

Where is the bus to the city?
Где автобус в город?
gd'yeh av-TOH-boos v GO-raht?

Where is the telephone?
Где телефон?
gd'yeh teh-leh-FOHN?

. . . the airport restaurant?
. . . ресторан в аэропорту?
. . . rest-ah-RAHN v a-eh-ra-pohr-TOO?

Porter! Take these bags to a taxi.
Носильщик! Отнесите эти чемоданы в такси.
na-SEEL'-sh'check! aht-n'yeh-SEET-yeh EH-tee cheh-mo-DA-nee f tahk-SEE.

I'll carry this one myself.
Я понесу этот сам.
ya pa-n'yeh-SOO EH-taht sam.

Taxi!
Такси!
tahk-SEE!

To the Moskva Hotel . . .
В гостиницу Москва . . .
v ga-STEE-neet-soo mahsk-VA . . .

How much does it cost?
Сколько стоит?
SKOHL-ka STO-yeet?

Do you speak English?
Вы говорите по-английски?
vwee ga-VA-REE-t'yeh pa-ahn-GLEE-skee?

I speak only a little Russian.
Я немного говорю по-русски.
ya n'yeh MNO-ga GA-var-YOO pa-ROOSS-kee.

Do you understand?
Вы понимаете?
vwee pa-nee-MA-yet-yeh?

I understand.
Я понимаю.
ya pa-nee-MA-yoo.

I don't understand.
Я не понимаю.
ya n'yeh pa-nee-MA-yoo.

Speak slowly.
Говорите медленно.
*ga-va-REET-yeh
  m'YED-len-na.*

Repeat, please.
Повторите, пожа-
  луйста.
*pahv-ta-REET-yeh,
  pa-ZHAHL-sta.*

Write it down.
Запишите.
za-pee-SHEET-t'yeh.

Who is it?
Кто это?
ktoh EH-tah?

Come in!
Войдите!
voy-DEET-yeh!

Don't come in!
Не входите!
n'yeh v'ha-DEET-yeh!

Wait, please.
Подождите, пожалу-
  йста.
*pa-dahzh-DEET-yeh,
  pa-ZHAHL'-sta.*

Let's go!
Идемте!
ee-d'YOM-t'yeh!

That's all.
Это всё.
EH-toh fs'yo.

What is this?
Что это?
sh'toh EH-ta?

Where's the telephone?
Где телефон?
gd'yeh teh-leh-FOHN?

Where is the men's room?	**...ladies' room?**
Где мужской туалет?	...дамский туалет?
gd'yeh moosh-SKOY twa-LET?	*...DAHM-skee twahl-YET?*

Note: Russian is simple (in some ways). There is no word for "the," and no word for "a" or "an," except the number "one" (*один*) when specifically is called for.

Show me, please.
Покажите мне, пожалуйста.
pa-ka-ZHEET-yeh m'n'yeh, pa-ZHAHL'-sta.

Excuse me, where is...?	**...the American Consulate?**
Извините, где...?	...американское консульство?
Eez-vee-NEET-yeh, gd'yeh...?	*...ah-meh-ree-KAHN-ska-yeh KOHN-soolst-va?*

...British...	**...Canadian...**
...английское...	...канадское...
...ahn-GLEE-ska-yeh...	*...ka-NAHD-ska-yeh...*

...a hospital?	**...a pharmacy?**	**...the subway?**
...больница?	...аптека?	...метро?
...bahl'-NEE-tsa?	*...ahp-T'YEH-ka?*	*...meh-TRO?*

...a department store?	**...a movie theater?**
...универмаг?	...кинотеатр?
...oo-neh-vehr-MAHG?	*...kee-no-teh-AHTR?*

. . . a good restaurant?
. . . хороший ресторан?
. . . *ha-RO-shee res-tah-RAHN?*

You are very kind.
Вы очень добры.
vwee OH-chen' da-BREE.

Many thanks.
Большое спасибо.
bahl-SHO-yeh
    spa-SEE-ba.

This is Red Square.
Это Красная Площадь.
EH-ta KRAHS-na-ya PLO-sh'chat.

What is that building?
Какое это здание?
ka-KO-yeh EH-toh Z'DA-nee-yeh?

It's St. Basil's cathedral.
Это Собор Василия Блаженного.
EH-ta sa-BOR va-SEE-lee-ya bla-ZHEN-na-va.

This is Lenin's tomb.
Это мавзолей Ленина.
EH-ta mav-za-LAY LEH-nee-na.

Over there is the Kremlin.
Вот там Кремль.
voht tahm KREHML'.

Where is the Winter Palace?
Где Зимний дворец?
gd'yeh ZEEM-nee dva-R'YETS?

It's not in Moscow.
Это не в Москве.
EH-ta n'yeh v'mahs-
K'VEH.

It's in St. Petersburg.
Это в Петербурге.
EH-ta f' pee-t'yehr-
BOORG-'yeh.

5. Hotel—Laundry— Dry Cleaning

Although the staffs of the larger hotels have some training in English, you will find that the use of Russian makes for better understanding and better relations, especially with the service personnel. We have included laundry and dry cleaning in this section so you can make yourself understood in speaking to the hotel chambermaid or valet.

Good day. I have a reservation.
Добрый день. У меня есть бронь.
DOH-bree d'yen'. oo men-YA yest' bron'.

My name is...
Меня зовут...
men-YA za-VOOT...

I would like...
Я хотел бы...
ya ha-T'YEL bwee...

...a single room.
...отдельный номер.
...oht-d'YEL'-nee NO-mer.

...with two beds.
...с двумя кроватями.
...z' dvoom-YA kra-VAHT-ya-mee.

...with bath.
...с ванной.
...s' VA-noy.

Not too expensive.
Не слишком дорого.
n'yeh SLISH-kom DOH-ra-ga.

Is there a radio?
С радио?
s' RA-dio?

...television?
...с телевизором?
...s' tel-eh-VEE-za-ram?

How much is it?
Сколько стоит?
SKOHL'ka STO-eet?

One day.
Один день.
ah-DEEN d'yen'.

One week.
Одна неделя.
ahd-NA neh-D'YEL-ya.

May I see it?
Можно это посмотреть?
Mo-zhna EH-ta pa-sma-TR'YET'?

Is breakfast included?
Завтрак включен?
ZAHV-trak v-klyoo-CHOHN?

Where is the bathroom?
Где туалет?
g'd'yeh twa-LET?

...the shower?
...душ?
....doosh?

I need a different room.
Мне нужен другой номер.
mn'yeh NOOZH-en droo-GOY NO-mer.

Better.
Лучше.
LOOT-sheh.

Larger.
Больше.
BOHL'-sheh.

This one I like.
Этот номер мне
  подходит.
*EH-taht NO-mer mnyeh
  pad-HOH-dit.*

I'll stay five days.
Я пробуду пять дней.
*ya pra-BOO-doo p'yaht'
  dn'yey.*

Perhaps a week.
Может быть, одну неделю.
MO-zhet bweet' ad-NOO n'yeh-D'YEL-yoo.

**When do you serve
  lunch?**
Когда обед?
kahg-DA ahb-YET?

...dinner?
...ужин?
...OO-zheen?

Please...
Пожалуйста...
*pa-ZHAHL'-
  sta...*

**...mineral
  water.**
...минераль-
  ная.
*...mee-neh-
  RAHL'-na-ya.*

...ice.
...лёд.
...l'yohd.

Breakfast for room 405.
Завтрак для номера четыреста пять.
*ZAHV-trak d'l'ya NO-meh-ra cheh-TEE-r'yes-ta
  p'yaht'.*

Coffee with milk, rolls, and butter.
Кофе с молоком, булочки и масло.
KO-f'yeh s' ma-la-KOM, BOO-lahtch-kee ee MA-sla.

My key, please.
Мой ключ, пожалуйста.
moy klooch, pa-ZHAHL-sta.

Is there a letter for me?
Есть ли письмо для меня?
yest' lee pee-SMO dl'ya men-YA?

Please, send these letters.
Пожалуйста, пошлите эти письма.
pa-ZHAHL-sta, pa-SLEET-yeh EH-tee PEES'-ma.

Will you put stamps on them, please?
Приклейте марки на них, пожалуйста?
pree-KLAY-t'yeh MAR-kee na nikh, pa-ZHAHL-sta?

I want to speak with the manager.
Я хочу говорить с администратором.
*ya ha-CHOO ga-va-REET'
s' ahd-mee-nee-STRA-ta-rahm.*

I need an interpreter.
Мне нужен переводчик.
mn'yeh NOOZH-en p'yeh-reh-VOHD-chik.

Are you the chambermaid?
Вы горничная?
vwee GOR-neech-na-ya?

I need...
Мне нужно...
m'n'yeh NOOZH-na...

...a blanket.
...одеяло.
...ahd-yeh-YA-la.

...a pillow.
...подушка.
...pa-DOOSH-ka.

...a towel.
...полотенце.
...pa-la-T'YEN-t'seh.

...soap.
...мыло.
...*MWEE-la.*

...toilet paper.
...туалетная бумага.
...*t'wa-LET-na-ya
boo-MA-ga.*

This is for cleaning.
Это для чистки.
EH-ta dl'ya CHEEST-kee.

This is for pressing only.
Это для глажки только.
EH-ta dl'ya GLASH-kee TOHL'ka.

This is for washing.
Это для стирки.
EH-ta dl'ya v'STEER-kee.

Can this be repaired?
Можно ли это
  отремонтировать?
*MOHZH-na lee EH-ta
  aht-reh-mahn-TEE-
  ra-vaht'?*

This evening?
Сегодня вечером?
*seh-VOHD-n'ya
  VEH-cheh-rahm?*

...tomorrow?
...завтра?
...*ZAHV-tra?*

...tomorrow afternoon?
...завтра после обеда?
...*ZAHV-tra PO-slee ab-
  YEH-da?*

...tomorrow evening?
...завтра вечером?
...*ZAHV-tra
  VEH-cheh-rahm?*

Be careful with this.
Будьте осторожны с
  этим.
*BOOD-t'yeh
  ah-sta-ROHZH-nee
  s' EH-teem.*

When will it be ready?
Когда будет готово?
kahg-DA BOOD-yet ga-TOH-va?

Are you sure?
Вы уверены?
vwee oo-V'YEH-reh-nee?

Is it ready now?
Уже готово?
oo-ZHE ga-TOH-va?

The bill, please?
Счёт, пожалуйста.
sh'choht, pa-ZHAHL'-sta.

I'm leaving tomorrow morning.
Я уезжаю завтра утром.
Ya oo-ye-ZHA-yoo ZAHF-tra OO-trahm.

Please call me at seven A.M.
Позвоните мне в семь часов утра.
pa-zvo-NEE-t'yeh mn'yeh f' syem' cha-SOHF OO-tra.

It's very important.
Это очень важно.
EH-ta OH-chen VAHZH-na.

When is checkout time?
Когда нужно освободить номер?
kahg-DA NOOZH-na as-va-ba-DEET' NO-mehr?

Point to the Answer

To make sure you understand the answer to your question show the following section to a Russian-speaking person so he or she can select the answer. The sentence in Russian after the arrow asks him or her point to the answer. Other "Point to the Answer" sections appear on later pages.

Укажите, пожалуйста ваш ответ на мой вопрос на следующей странице. Большое спасибо.

сегодня today	**сегодня вечером** this evening	**завтра** tomorrow

рано early	**поздно** late

час—1 o'clock	шесть часов—6 o'clock
два часа—2 o'clock	семь часов—7 o'clock
три часа—3 o'clock	восемь часов—8 o'clock
четыре часа—4 o'clock	девять часов—9 o'clock
пять часов—5 o'clock	

десять часов—10 o'clock
одиннадцать часов—11 o'clock
двенадцать часов—12 o'clock

Понедельник Monday	**Вторник** Tuesday	**Среда** Wednesday	**Четверг** Thursday

Пятница Friday	**Суббота** Saturday	**Воскресенье** Sunday

Note: For pronunciation of days of the week, see the next chapter.

6. Time: Hours—Days—Months

In the "Hotel" section you noted that when making an appointment at a certain hour you simply put **v'** in front of the number followed by час (**chass**)—"hour." The following section tells you how to tell time in greater detail, including dates. You can make all sorts of arrangements with people by indicating the hour, the day, the date, and adding *ha-ra-SHO lee EH-ta?*—"Is that good?" or "O.K.?"

What time is it?	**It's one o'clock.**	**six o'clock.**
Который час?	Один час.	шесть часов.
ka-TOH-ree chahs?	*ah-DEEN chahs.*	*shest' cha-SOHF.*

Half past six.
Половина седьмого.
pa-la-VEE-na s'yed-MO-va.

Fifteen minutes past seven.
Пятнадцать минут восьмого.
p'yaht-NAHT-tsaht' mee-NOOT vahs-MO-va.

24

A quarter to eight.
Без четверти восемь.
*b'yez CHET-vyer-tee
   VO-s'yem'.*

Ten minutes past ten.
Десять минут
   одиннадцатого.
*d'YEH-sit' mee-NOOT ah-
   DEEN-NAHT-tsa-ta-va.*

At nine o'clock.
В девять часов.
*v' D'YEHV-yaht' cha-
   SOHF.*

Exactly ten o'clock.
Ровно десять часов.
*ROHV-na d'YEH-s'yaht'
   cha-SOHF.*

In the morning.
Утром.
OO-trahm.

noon	evening	night
полдень	вечером	ночь
POHL-d'yen'	*VYEH-cher-ohm*	*nohch'*

today	yesterday	the day before yesterday
сегодня	вчера	позавчера
seh-VOHD-n'ya	*fcheh-RA*	*pa-za-fcheh-RA.*

till tomorrow
до завтра
da ZAHV-tra

the day after tomorrow
послезавтра
pa-sleh-ZAHV-tra

Good morning!	Good evening!	Good night!
Доброе утро!	Добрый вечер!	Спокойной ночи!
DOH-bro-yeh OO-tra!	*DOH-bree VYEH-cher!*	*spa-KOY-nay NO-chee!*

last night
вчера вечером
v'cheh-RA
  VEH-cheh-
  rahm

two weeks ago
две недели тому
  назад
d'veh n'yeh-
  DEH-lee
  ta-MOO
  na-ZAHT

next week
следующая
  неделя
SLEH-d'yoo-sha-
  ya n'yeh-
  D'YEH-l'ya

this month
этот месяц
EH-taht M'YEH-s'yahts

next month
следующий месяц
SLEH-d'yoo-shee M'YEH-
  s'yahts

several months ago
несколько месяцев
  назад
N'YEH-skohl'-ka
  m'yeh-s'yeht-sef
  na-ZAHD

this year
этот год
EH-taht goht

last year
прошлый год
PRO-shlee goht

next year
следующий год
SLEH-d'yoo-
  shee goht

five years ago
пять лет тому
  назад
p'yaht' l'yet
  ta-MOO
  na-ZAHT

Monday
Понедельник
pahn-yeh-
  D'YEL-neek

Tuesday
Вторник
F'TOR-neek

Wednesday
Среда
sreh-DA

Thursday
Четверг
chet-VERK

Friday
Пятница
PYAHT-nee-tsa

Saturday
Суббота
Soo-BOH-ta

Sunday
Воскресенье
va-skreh-S'YEHN-yeh

next Monday
следующий
  понедельник
SLEH-d'yoo-shee
  pahn-yeh-d'YEL'-neek

every Sunday
каждое воскресенье
KAZH-do-yeh
  va-skreh-S'YEHN-yeh

last Tuesday
прошлый вторник
PRO-shlee F'TOR-neek

until Friday
до пятницы
da P'YAHT-nee-tsi

January
январь
yahn-VAR

February
февраль
fev-RAL'

March
март
mart

April
Апрель
ahp-R'YEHL'

May
май
my

June
июнь
ee'YOON'

July
июль
yool'

August
август
AHV-goost

September
сентябрь
s'yen-T'YA-br'

October
октябрь
ahk-T'YA-br'

November
ноябрь
na-YA-br'

December
декабрь
deh-KA-br'

What's the date?
Какое число?
ka-KO-ye chee-SLO?

The first of May.
Первое мая.
PEHR-vo-yeh MA-ya.

What year?
Какой год?
ka-KOY goht?

1992
тысяча девятьсот
   девяносто второй
TEE-s'yeh-cha
   d'yeh-veht-SOHT
   d'yeh-ve-NO-sta
   f'ta-ROY

Today is a holiday...
Сегодня праздник...
s'yeh-VOHD-n'ya
   PRAHZ-dnik...

...the first of January.
...первое января.
...P'YEHR-voe
   yahn-vahr-YA.

To the New Year!
С Новым Годом!
s' NO-vim GO-dahm!

When is your birthday?
Когда ваш день
   рождения?
kahk-DA vahsh d'yen'
   rahzh-D'YEN'-ee-ya?

I congratulate you!
Я поздравляю вас!
ya pahz-dra-VL'YA-yoo vahss!

7. Money

This section contains the vocabulary necessary for changing money. The currency is the "ruble" (*рубль*) and the abbreviation for ruble is руб. and the plural is рублей (roo-BLAY). You may have heard of the black market—*чёрный рынок* (CH'YOR-nee REE-nok), but approach this with caution. Purchase in the dollar stores. It's safer!

Where can I change dollars?

Где я могу обменять доллары?

gd'yeh ya ma-GOO ahb-m'yen-YAHT' DOH-la-ree?

Pounds?

Фунты?

FOON-tee?

Can I change money here?

Могу ли я обменять здесь деньги?

ma-GOO lee ya ahb-m'yen-YAHT' zd'yes' D'YEN'-ghee?

When is the bank open?
Когда банк открыт?
kahg-DA bahnk aht-KREET?

In ten minutes.
Через десять минут.
CHEH-rez D'YEH-s'yaht' mee-NOOT.

What is the rate?   **... rubles to the dollar.**
Какой курс?   ... рублей за доллар.
ka-KOY koors?   *... roo-BLAY za*
                                          DOH-lar.

I want to change $100.00.
Я хочу обменять сто долларов.
ya ha-CHOO ab-m'yen-YAHT' sto DOH-la-rof.

Do you accept travelers' checks?
Принимаете ли вы международные чеки?
*pree-nee-MA-yeh-t'yeh lee vwee mezh-doo-na-ROHD-
nee-yeh CHEH-kee?*

Very sorry. Not here.
Очень жаль. Не здесь.
OH-chen' zhahl. N'yeh zd'yes.

Can you accept my check?
Можете ли вы принять мой чек?
MO-zhe-t'yeh lee vwee pree-N'YAHT' moy check?

Have you identification?
У вас есть удостоверение?
oo vahss yest' oo-da-sta-veh-REH-nee-yeh?

Of course.
Конечно.
kahn-YETCH-na.

Here is my passport.
Вот мой паспорт.
voht moy PAHS-port.

Please give me five tens nine fives.
Пожалуйста, дайте мне пять десяток, десять
   пятёрок.
*pa-ZHAHL'-sta, D'YE-t'yeh mn'yeh p'yaht' d'yehs-YA-
   tahk, D'YEH-s'yaht' p'ya-T'YO-rahk.*

and the rest in change.
и остальное мелочью.
ee ah-stal-NO-yeh M'YEH-lahch-yoo.

I need small change.
Мне нужна мелочь.
mn'yeh noozh-NA M'YEH-lahch.

8. Basic Foods

The foods and drinks mentioned in this section will enable you to be well-fed on your travels in Russia. The section that follows this one deals with special regional dishes, representative of the tasty and substantial cuisines of the different members of the Commonwealth of Independent States.

Breakfast	orange juice
Завтрак	апельсиновый сок
ZAHF-trahk	*ah-pehl'-SEE-no-vee sohk*

boiled eggs	fried eggs	scrambled eggs (omelet)
варёные яйца	яичница	омлет
vah-R'YO-nee-yeh YAI-tsa	*ya-EESH-nee-tsa*	*ahm-l'YET*

omlet	with ham	with bacon
омлет	с ветчиной	с беконом
ahm-L'YET	*s' veht-chee-NOY*	*s' BAY-ka-nahm*

rolls
булочки
BOO-latch-kee

toast
гренки
GR'YEN-kee

coffee with milk
кофе с молоком
KO-f'yeh s' ma-la-KOHM

tea with lemon
чай с лимоном
chai s' lee-MO-nahm

lunch
второй завтрак
*v'ta-ROY
 ZAHF-trahk*

**dinner (usually
 served mid-
 day)**
обед
ah-B'YED

**supper (usually
 served in eve-
 ning)**
ужин
OO-zhin

Please, tell me . . .
Скажите мне, пожалуйста . . .
ska-ZHEET-yeh mn'yeh pa-ZHAHL'-sta.

Where is there a good restaurant?
Где хороший ресторан?
gd'yeh ha-RO-shee res-ta-RAHN?

A table for three.
Столик на троих.
STO-leek na tra-EEKH.

Follow me, please.
Следуйте за мной.
*SLEH-doo-eet-yeh za
 M'NOY.*

The menu, please.
Меню, пожалуйста.
*mehn-YOO,
 pa-ZAHL'-sta.*

What is this?
Что это?
sh'toh EH-tah?

This for me.
Это для меня.
EH-toh dl'ya men-YA.

First, a cocktail.
Сначала коктейль.
sna-CHA-la, kok-TAIL'.

Then an ap- petizer.	caviar	salmon
Затем закуски.	икра	лосось
za-T'YEM za-KOOS-kee.	ee-KRA	la-SOHS'

herring	salad	salt	oil	vinegar
селёдка	салат	соль	масло	уксус
seh- L'YOHT- ka	sa-LAHT	sohl'	MA-sla	OOK-soos

chicken	roast beef	steak	raw
цыплёнок	ростбиф	бифштекс	сырой
tsip-L'YO- nak	ROHST-beef	beef-SHTEX	see-ROY

rare	well done	roast pork
слегка прижаренный	хорошо прожаренный	свиное жаркое
slek-KA pree-ZHA- ren-nee	ha-ra-SHO pra-ZHA- ren-nee	svee-NO-yeh zhar-KO-yeh

beef	sausage
отбивные	колбаса
aht-beev-NEE-yeh	kahl-ba-SA

fish	duck
рыба	утка
REE-ba	OOT-ka

bread	butter	salt	pepper
хлеб	масло	соль	перец
hlep	MA-sla	sohl'	PEH-rets

fried potatoes	boiled potatoes	mashed potatoes
жареная	варёная	пюре
картошка	картошка	p'yoo-RAY
ZHA-reh-na-ya	var-YO-na-ya	
kar-TOHSH-ka	kar-TOHSH-ka	

mushrooms	peas	beans
грибы	горох	бобы
gree-BEE	ga-ROKH	ba-BWEE

spinach	carrots	onions	cucumber
шпинат	морковь	лук	огурец
shpee-NAHT	mar-KOF'	lewk	ah-goo-RETS

red wine	white wine	beer	vodka
красное вино	белое вино	пиво	водка
KRA-sna-yeh vee-NO	B'YEL-a-yeh vee-NO	PEE-va	VOHD-ka

To your health!
За ваше здоровье!
za VA-sheh zda-RO-v'yeh!

fruit	grape	apple
фрукты	виноград	яблоко
FROOK-tee	vee-na-GRAHT	YA-bla-ka

orange	juice
апельсин	сок
ah-pehl'-SEEN	sohk

dessert	pastry	cake	cheese
сладкое	пирожное	торт	сыр
SLAHT-ko-yeh	pee-ROZH-na-yeh	tort	seer

ice cream	coffee	sugar	cream
мороженое	кофе	сахар	сливки
ma-RO-zheh-na-yeh	*KO-f'yeh*	*SA-khar*	*SLEEV-kee*

More, please.
Еще, пожалуйста.
*yesh-CHO,
pa-ZHAHL'-sta.*

That's enough.
Это достаточно.
EH-ta da-STA-tahtch-na.

Waitress!
Официантка!
aht-feet-SAHN-ka!

Waiter!
Официант!
ah-feet-SAHNT!

The check, please.
Счёт, пожалуй-
ста.
*shch'yoht, pa-
ZHAHL'-sta.*

Is the tip included?
Включены ли чаевые?
f-klyoo-cheh-NEE lee cha-yeh-VWEE-yeh?

Excuse me, I think the bill is wrong.
Извините, я думаю, счёт неправильный.
*eez-vee-NEE-t'yeh, ya DOO-ma-yoo, sh'ch'yoht n'yeh
PRA-veel'-nee.*

Oh, no.
О, нет.
oh, n'yet.

Look here.
Посмотрите.
*pa-sma-TREE-
t'yeh.*

You see?
Вы видите?
*Vwee VEE-dee-
t'yeh?*

Oh, yes. That's right.
О, да. Это правильно.
*oh, da. EH-ta PRA-vil'-
na.*

Everything is O.K.
Всё в порядке.
fs'yo f pa-R'YAHD-keh.

and you may hear the reply . . .

Come again soon!
Приходите снова!
pree-ha-DEET-yeh SNO-va!

Point to the Answer

Show the following section to a Russian-speaking person so that he or she can select the pertinent answer by pointing to it below. The paragraph in Russian after the arrow asks him (or her) to do this.

Укажите, пожалуйста, ваш ответ на мой вопрос на следующей странице. Большое спасибо.

Это наше специальное блюдо.
This is our special dish.

Это готово.
It's ready.

Это не готово.
It's not ready.

Это займёт _____ минут.
It will take _____ minutes.

У нас нет этого сегодня.
We don't have it today.

Только по пятницам.
Only on Fridays.

Это . . .
It's . . .

цыплёнок
chicken

свинина
pork

баранина	телятина	говядина
lamb	veal	beef

колбаса	ветчина	рыба
sausage	ham	fish

с овощами	с соусом
with vegetables	with a sauce

9. Food Specialties of Russia and Associated Countries

Hot pancakes with caviar.
Блины с икрой.
blee-NEE s'eek-ROY.

borscht
борщ
borshch

beef stroganoff
биф-строганов
beef-STRO-ga-nahf
[beef, egg, sour cream, dill, garlic, onion]

fish with sour cream
рыба в сметане
REE-ba f smeh-TA-neh

shaslik
шашлык
shahsh-LEEK
[meat roasted on skewers)

What is this wine?
Какое это вино?
ka-KO-yeh eh-ta vee-NO?

It's from Georgia.
Это из Грузии.
EH-ta eez GROO-zee-ee.

Do you like it?
Вам нравится?
vahm N'RA-veet-s'ya?

It's excellent.
Это отлично.
EH-ta aht-LEECH-na!

Do you like vodka?
Вы любите водку?
vwee L'YOO-beet-yeh VOHD-koo?

Certainly!
Конечно!
kahn-YETCH-na!

To your health!
За ваше здоровье!
za VA-sheh zda-ROHV-yeh!

Thank you for a fine dinner!
Спасибо за прекрасный обед!
spa-SEE-ba za pree-KRAHS-nee nee ab-YET!

You are welcome!
Добро пожаловать!
da-BRO pa-zha-lo-VAHT'!

I'm happy you enjoyed it!
Я рад, вам это понравилось!
ya rahd, vahm EH-ta pahn-N'RA-vee-lahs'!

10. Transportation

Getting around by public transportation is enjoyable not only for the new and interesting things you see but also because of the opportunities you have for practicing Russian. To make your travels easier, use short phrases when speaking to drivers or others when you ask directions. And don't forget "Please" / пожалуйста (*pa-ZHAHL'-sta*) and "Thank you" / спасибо (*spa-SEE-ba*).

Bus

Bus
автобус
ahf-TOH-boos

Where is the bus stop?
Где автобусная
    остановка?
*gd'yeh ahf-TO-boo-sna-ya
    ah-sta-NOHF-ka?*

Do you go to _____ ?
Вы идёте до _____ ?
vwee eed-YO-t'yeh doh _____ ?

No. Take number nine.
Нет. Сядьте на номер девять.
n'yet. S'YA-t'yeh na NO-mer D'YEHV-yaht'.

How much is the fare?
Сколько стоит билет?
SKOHL'-ka STO-eet bee-L'YET?

Where do you want to go?
Куда вы хотите попасть?
koo-DA vwee ha-TEET-yeh pa-PAHST'?

To the Kremlin.
В Кремль.
f krehml'.

Is it far?
Это далеко?
EH-ta dal'yeh-KO?

No. It's near.
Нет. Это близко.
n'yet. EH-ta BLEEZ-ka.

Please, tell me where to get off.
Пожалуйста, скажите мне, где выходить.
*pa-ZHAHL'-sta, ska-ZHEET-yeh mn'yeh, gd'yeh vwee-
    ha-DEET'.*

Gett off here.
Выходите здесь.
vwee-kha-DEET'yeh zd'yes'.

Point to the Answer

Show the following section to a Russian-speaking person
so he or she can select the answer. The section in Russian

following the arrow asks the Russian person to point to the answer.

Укажите, пожалуйста, ваш ответ на мой вопрос на следующей странице. Большое спасибо.

Там.
Over there.

В этом направлении.
This direction.

Я не знаю.
I don't know.

На другой стороне улицы.
On the other side of the street.

На углу.
At the corner.

Направо.
To the right.

Налево.
To the left.

Прямо.
Straight ahead.

Это близко.
It's near.

Вы можете пройти туда.
You can walk there.

В этом направлении.
It's that way.

Это далеко.
It's far.

Возьмите такси.
Take a taxi.

Используйте метро.
Take the subway.

или используйте автобус номер _____
or, take bus no. _____

Taxi

Taxi!
Такси!
tahk-SEE!

Are you free?
Вы свободны?
*vwee-sva-
BO-d'nee?*

**This is the ad-
dress.**
Это адрес.
eh-ta AH-dres.

Do you know where it is?
Знаете ли вы, где это?
*ZNA-yeh-t'yeh lee vwee
gd'yeh EH-ta?*

I'm in a hurry.
Я спешу.
ya speh-SHOO.

Go fast!
Быстро!
BWEE-stra!

Hurry!
Скорее!
ska-REH-yeh!

Slow down!
Медленнее!
*MED-len-neh-
yeh!*

Stop here!
Остановитесь здесь!
*ah-sta-na-VEE-t'yes'
zd'yes'!*

At the corner.
На углу.
na oo-GLOO.

Wait for me.
Подождите меня.
*pa-da-zh'DEE-t'yeh
meen-YA.*

O.K.?
Хорошо?
ha-ra-SHO?

I'll be back soon.
Я скоро вернусь.
ya SKO-ra vehr-NOOS'.

In five minutes.
Через пять минут.
*CHEH-res' p'yaht' min-
OOT.*

How much is it per hour?	...**kilometer?**
	...**километр?**
Сколько стоит час?	...*kee-la-M'YETR?*
SKOHL'ka STO-eet chas?	

What's the matter?
Что случилось?
Sh'toh sloo-CHEE-lahs?

Point to the Answer

To make sure you understand the taxi driver's answer to your question, show your driver the following section so he or she can select the answer. The sentence in Russian after the arrow asks him or her to point to the answer.

 Укажите, пожалуйста, ваш ответ на мой вопрос на следующей странице. Большое спасибо.

Я подожду вас здесь.
I will wait here for you.

Я вернусь за вами.
I'll come back to pick you up.

Я не могу ждать. Я не могу парковаться здесь.
I can't wait. I can't park here.

У меня нет мелочи.
I can't change that bill.

Subway

Is there a subway in this city?
Есть ли метро в городе?
yest' lee met-RO v' GO-ra-deh?

Where is the subway?
Где метро?
gd'yeh met-RO?

What is the fare?
Сколько стоит?
SKOHL'-ka STO-eet?

Where do I change trains?
Где я делаю пересадку?
gd'yeh ya d'YEH-la-YOO peh-reh-SAHD-koo?

I'm going to _____ .
Я еду до _____ .
ya YEH-doo doh _____ .

Train

Where is the train station?
Где вокзал?
gd'yeh vahk-ZAHL?

Where can I buy tickets?
Где я могу купить билет?
gd'yeh ya ma-GOO koo-PEET' bee-L'YET?

One ticket for Odessa.
Один билет до Одессы.
ah-DEEN beel-YET doh ahd-YES-see.

Round trip.
Туда и обратно.
too-DA ee ah-BRAHT-na.

One way.
Туда.
too-DA.

Soft (First class)
Мягкий вагон
M'YAKH-kee va-GOHN

Hard (Second class)
Жёсткий вагон
ZHOST-kee va-GOHN

When does it leave?
Когда отходит?
kahg-DA oht-HO-deet?

Is this seat taken?
Это место занято?
EH-ta m'YES-ta ZAHN-ya-ta?

It's free.
Свободно.
sva-BO-dna.

You may sit here.
Вы можете сесть здесь.
vwee MO-zheh-t'yeh s'yest zd'yes.

At what time do we get to Odessa?
Когда мы приезжаем в Одессу?
kahg-DA mwee pree-yeh-ZHA-yem v' ahd-YES-soo?

Does the train stop in Nizhny Novgorod?
Поезд останавливается в Нижнем Новгороде?
POH-yest ah-sta-NAHV-lee-va-yet-sa v' NIZH-neem NOHV-ga-ra-de?

Where is the dining car?
Где вагон-ресторан?
gd'yeh va-GOHN res-ta-RAHN?

I can't find...	...my ticket.	...my baggage.
Я не могу найти...	...мой билет.	...мой багаж.
ya-n'yeh *ma-GOO* *nai-TEE...*	*...moy beel-YEHT.*	*...moy ba-GASH.*

Can you help me?
Вы можете мне помочь?
vwee MO-zhet-yeh mn'yeh pa-MOHCH ?

I took the wrong train.
Я сел не в тот поезд.
ya s'yel n'yeh f toht POH-yest.

I want to go to Minsk.
Я хочу поехать в Минск.
ya ha-CHOO pa-YEH-haht' v Meensk.

Point to the Answer

To make sure that you understand the answer to your question, show the following section to the conductor or station guard so he or she can select the answer. The sentence in Russian asks him or her to point to the answer.

Укажите, пожалуйста, ваш ответ на мой вопрос на следующей странице. Большое спасибо.

Путь номер _____ .	В том направлении.
Track number	That way.

_____ .

Внизу
Downstairs

Наверху
Upstairs.

Поезд отходит через пять минут.
The train leaves in five minutes.

Вы должны сделать пересадку в _____ .
You must change at _____ .

Мы приезжаем в семь пятнадцать.
We arrive at 7:15.

Ship

What time does the ship sail?
Когда отплывает пароход ?
kahg-DA aht-plee-VAH-yet pa-ra-KHOHT?

At what ports does it stop?
В каких портах пароход останавливается?
*f ka-KEEKH por-TAHKH pa-ra-KHOHT o-sta-NA-vlee-
VA-yet-sa?*

Where is my cabin?
Где моя каюта?
*gd'YEH ma-YA ka-YOO-
ta?*

Number 101.
Номер сто один.
NO-mer sto ah-DEEN.

Where is my baggage?
Где мой багаж?
gd'yeh moy ba-GAHZH?

Where is the bar?   **...the dining room?**
Где бар?   ...столовая?
gd'yeh bar?   *...sta-LO-va-ya?*

What are those people singing?
Что эти люди поют?
sh-toh EH-tee L'YOO-dee pa-YOOT?

It's about the Volga...   **our Russian river.**
Это о Волге...   наша русская река.
EH-ta ah VOHL-g'yeh...   *NA-sha ROOS-ka-ya*
                                 r'yeh-KA.

The song is called "Stenka Razin."
Песня называется «Стенька Разин»
P'YES-n'ya na-zee-VA-yet-s'ya STEN-ka RA-zin.

11. Trips by Car

Where can I rent a car here?
Где можно взять напрокат автомобиль?
*Gd'yeh MO-zhna VZ'YAHT' na-pra-KAHT
ahf-ta-ma-BEEL?*

...a motorcycle?
...мотоцикл?
...mo-toh-T'SEEKL?

...a bicycle?
...велосипед?
...veh-la-see-P'YET?

How much per day?
Сколько стоит день?
SKOHL'ka STO-eet d'yen'?

How much per kilometer?
Сколько стоит километр?
SKOHL'ka STO-eet kee-la-M'YETR?

Is the gasoline included?
Включая бензин?
fkl'yoo-CHA-ya ben-ZEEN?

51

I would like to try it out.
Я хотел бы испробовать.
ya kha-T'YEL-bwee ees-PRO-ba-vaht'.

Gas Station

Where is the next gas station?
Где следующая бензоколонка?
gd'yeh SL'YEH-doo-yoo-sha-ya ben-zo-ka-LOHN-ka?

How much per liter?
Сколько стоит литр?
SKOHL'-ka STO-eet leetr?

Forty liters, please.
Сорок литров, пожалуйста.
SO-rahk LEET-rof, pa-ZHAHL'-sta.

Fill the tank.
Наполните бак.
na-POHL-nee-t'yeh bahk.

Check...	**...the tires.**
Проверьте...	...шины.
pra-V'YEHR'-t'yeh...	*...SHEE-nee.*
...the battery.	**...the brakes.**
...аккумулятор.	...тормоз.
...ah-ko-mool-YA-tor.	*...TOR-mahz.*
...the oil.	**...the carburator.**
...масло.	...карбюратор.
...MA-sla.	*...kar-b'yoo-RA-tor.*

Change this tire.
Смените эту шину.
smeh-NEE-t'yeh EH-too SHEE-noo.

Have you a road map?
У вас есть дорожная карта?
oo vahs yest' da-ROHZH-na-ya KAR-ta?

Asking Directions

Where does this road go?
Куда эта дорога идёт?
koo-DA EH-ta da-RO-ga eed-YOHT?

Is the road good?
Хороша ли дорога?
ha-ra-SHAH lee da-RO-ga?

Is this the road to Smolensk?
Это дорога на Смоленск?
EH-tah da-RO-ga na smo-L'YENSK?

Is the next town far?
Далеко ли следующий город?
dahl-yeh-KO lee SL'YEH-doo-shee GO-raht?

In this direction?
В этом направлении?
V'EH-tahm na-pra-v'LEH-ne-ee?

Is there a good restaurant there?
Есть ли там хороший ресторан?
yest' lee tahm ha-RO-shee res-ta-RAN?

...a good hotel?

...хорошая гостиница?

...ha-RO-sha-ya ga-STEE-neet-sa?

What is it called?

Как это называется?

kahk EH-ta na-zee-VA-yet-sa?

Point to the Answer

To make sure that you understand the answer to your questions about driving directions, show the following section to the person whom you are asking. The sentence in Russian after the arrow asks him or her to point to the answer.

 Укажите, пожалуйста, ваш ответ на мой вопрос на следующей странице. Большое спасибо.

Это называется
_____ .

It is called _____ .

Оставайтесь на этой дороге.

Stay on this road.

Примерно пятьдесят километров.

About fifty kilometers.

Вы здесь на карте.

You are here on this map.

Поверните налево на следующем перекрестке.

Turn left at the next intersection.

Поверните направо у светофора.

Turn right at the traffic signal.

Затем следуйте прямо.
Then go straight ahead.

Следуйте по дороге на Рязань.
Take the road to Ryazan.

Но будьте осторожны.
But be careful.

Здесь ограничение скорости.
There is a speed limit.

Emergencies and Repairs

Your license, please.
Ваши права, пожалуйста.
VA-shee pra-VA, pa-ZHAHL'-sta.

Here it is.
Вот.
voht.

Also the car registration.
Также паспорт на машину.
TAHK-zheh PAS-port na ma-SHEE-noo.

It was not my fault.
Это не моя вина.
EH-ta n'yeh ma-YA vee-NA.

The truck hit my car.
Грузовик толкнул меня.
groo-za-VEEK talk-NOOL men-YA.

It's his fault.
Он виноват.
ohn vee-na-VAHT.

He drives too fast.
Он ездит слишком быстро.
ohn YEHZ-deet SLISH-kahm BWEE-stra.

I have a problem.
У меня проблема.
oo meh-N'YAH pra-BL'YEH-ma.

My car won't go.
Моя машина сломана.
ma-YA ma-SHEE-na SLO-ma-na.

Can you help me?
Можете ли вы помочь мне?
MO-zheh-t'yeh lee vwee poo-MOHCH mn'yeh?

I have a flat tire.
У меня спущено колесо.
oo men-YA SPOO-sh'cheh-na ka-leh-SO.

Can you lend me a jack?
Можете ли вы одолжить мне домкрат?
MO-zhe-t'yeh lee vwee ah-dahl-ZHEET' mn'yeh dahm-KRAT?

Can you push my car?
Можете ли вы подтолкнуть машину?
MO-zhe-t'yeh lee vwee paht-talk-KNOOT' ma-SHEE-noo?

Thank you very much.
Большое спасибо.
bahl'-SHOY-yeh spa-SEE-ba.

You are very kind.
Вы очень любезны.
vee OH-chen' l'yoo-B'YEZ-nee.

I need a mechanic.
Мне нужен механик.
mn'yeh NOO-zhen meh-HA-neek.

What's the matter?
Что случилось?
SHTOH sloo-CHEE-lahs'?

The motor is noisy.
Мотор шумит.
mo-TOR shoo-MEET.

It's hard to start.
Трудно завести.
TROOD-na za-ves-TEE.

Can you fix it?
Можете ли вы починить это?
MO-zhet-yeh lee vwee pa-chee-NEET' EH-ta?

I'm in a hurry.
Я спешу.
ya speh-SHOO.

What is the cost?
Сколько это будет стоить?
SKOHL'-ka EH-tah BOOD'-yet STOH-eet'?

How long will it take?
Как долго это будет?
kahk DOHL-ga EH-ta BOOD-yet?

Point to the Answer

To make sure that you understand the answers about car repair, show the following section to the mechanic so that he or she can point to the answer in Russian.

Укажите, пожалуйста, ваш ответ на мой вопрос на следующей странице. Большое спасибо.

Сегодня это невозможно.
Today it is not possible.

Возможно сегодня вечером.
Perhaps this evening.

Завтра.
Tomorrow.

Послезавтра.
The day after tomorrow.

Это будет стоить _____ рублей.
It will cost _____ rubles.

Это будет готово через ____ дней. ____ часов.
It will be ready in _____ days. ____ hours.

У нас нет деталей.
We don't have the parts.

Мы можем сделать это временно.
We can fix it temporarily.

Вам нужна новая покрышка.
You need a new tire.

Road Signs

You will also see or hear the following instructions:

Keep to the right	To the left	Detour
Направо	Налево	Объезд
na-PRA-va.	*na-L'YEH-va*	*ahb-YEZD*

One way
Одностороннее
  движение
ahd-na-sta-ROHN-
  n'yeh-yeh dvee-ZHEH-
  nee-yeh

Crossroads
Перекресток
peh-reh-KRYOHS-tahk

Speed limit 90 km
Предел скорости 90 километров
preh-D'YEL SKO-ra-stee 90 kee-la-MEH-trahf

No parking
Стоянка запрещена
sta-YAHN-ka za-preh-sh'cheh-NA

Road closed
Дорога закрыта
da-RO-ga za-KREE-ta

Railroad crossing
Переезд
p-yeh-r'yeh-YEZD

Exit
Выезд
VWEE-yehzd

International Road Signs

DANGER

CAUTION

SHARP TURN

CROSSROADS

RIGHT CURVE

LEFT CURVE

GUARDED RR CROSSING

UNGUARDED RR CROSSING

MAIN ROAD AHEAD

BUMPS

ONE WAY

DO NOT ENTER

NO PARKING

PARKING

12. Sightseeing and Photography

We have combined these two important sections, since you will want to take photographs of what you are seeing. Before you take a photograph be sure to ask a custodian. "Is it permitted?" Это разрешено? (**EH-ta rahz-reh-sheh-NO?**).

Sightseeing

I need a guide.
Мне нужен гид.
m'n'yeh NOO-zhen gheet.

Are you a guide?
Вы гид?
vwee gheet?

Do you speak English?
Вы говорите по-английски?
vwee ga-va-REET-yeh pa-ahn-GLEE-skee?

I speak a little Russian.
Я немного говорю по-русски.
ya n'yeh-M'NO-ga ga-vahr-YOO pa-ROOS-kee.

Do you have a car?
У вас есть машина?
oo vahs yest' ma-SHEE-na?

How much per hour?
Сколько стоит час?
SKOHL'-ka STO-eet chahs?

How much per day?
Сколько стоит день?
*SKOHL'-ka STO-eet
  d'yen'?*

For two people.
Для двух человек.
*dl'ya dvookh cheh-la-
  V'YEHK.*

We want to see
Мы хотим увидеть
*mwee kha-TEEM
  oo-VEED-yet'*

...the places of interest.
...достопримечатель-
ности.
*...da-sta-pree-meh-
  CHA-t'yel-na-stee.*

And, if you don't have a guide:

May one enter?
Можно войти?
MOHZH-na vai-TEE?

It is open.
Открыто.
aht-KREE-ta.

It is closed.
Закрыто.
za-KREE-ta.

May one take photographs?
Можно фотографировать?
MOHZH-na fa-ta-gra-FEE-ra-vaht?

It is permitted.
Это разрешено.
EH-ta rahz-reh-sheh-NO.

It is forbidden.
Это запрещено.
EH-ta za-preh-shcheh-NO.

Leave your packages here.
Оставьте ваши пакеты здесь.
a-STAHV-t'yeh VA-shee pa-KEH-tee zd'yess.

What is the admission?
Какая плата?
ka-KA-ya PLA-ta?

One ruble.
Один рубль.
ah-DEEN roobl.

And for children?
А для детей?
ah dl'ya dee-T'YEY?

It's free.
Бесплатно.
b'yehs-PLAHT-na.

We want to go
Мы хотим пойти
mwee kha-TEEM pa'-ee-TEE

...to the museum.
...в музей.
...v'moo-ZAY.

...to the park.
...в парк.
...f' park.

What is the name of
Как называется
kahk na-zee-VA-yet-s'ya

...this square?
эта площадь?
EH-ta PLO-sh'chat?

...this street?
...эта улица?
...EH-ta OO-leet-sa?

...this church?
...эта церковь?
...EH-ta TSEHR-kahf?

...this palace?
...этот дворец?
...EH-taht dva-RETS?

We want to see the city.
Мы хотим увидеть
  город.
mwee kha-TEEM oo-VEE-
d'yet GO-raht.

Very interesting!
Очень интересно!
Oh-chen' een-teh-
R'YES-na!

How beautiful!
Как красиво!
kahk kra-SEE-va!

When was this built?
Когда это было
  построено?
kahg-DA EH-ta BWEE-la
pahs-TRO-yeh-na?

Do you know a good
  nightclub?
Знаете ли вы хороший
  ночной клуб?
ZNA-yeh-t'yeh lee vwee
kha-RO-shee
nahtch-NOY kloop?

Let's go!
Пойдем!
pa-eed-YOHM!

You are a good guide.
Вы хороший гид.
vwee kha-RO-shee gheet.

Come again tomorrow.
Приходите завтра
  снова.
pree-ha-DEE-t'yeh
ZAHF-tra SNO-va.

At nine o'clock.
В девять часов.
v D'YEH-v'yaht cha-SOHF.

Here are some signs you may see in museums, palaces,
or public buildings:

MEN
мужская
MOOSH-ska-ya

WOMEN
женская
ZHEN-ska-ya

ENTRANCE
вход
fkhoht

EXIT
выход
VWEE-hoht

PUSH
от себя
oht seh-B'YA

PULL
к себе
k' seh-B'YEH

ON
включить
fkl'yoo-CHEET

OFF
выключить
VWEE-kl'yoo-cheet

COLD
холодно
KHO-la-dna

WARM
тепло
t'yeh-PLO

HOT
горячо
gahr-ya-CHO

VISITING HOURS
часы для посетителей
*cha-SEE dl'ya
   pa-seh-TEE-t'yehl-layh*

INFORMATION
информация
een-for-MA-tsee-ya

NO ADMISSION
не входить
n'yeh fkha-DEET

CHECKROOM
раздевалка
rahz-d'yeh-VAHL-ka

**SMOKING FORBID-
   DEN**
курить запрещено
*koo-REET
   za-presh-cheh-NO*

DANGER
опасно
ah-PA-sna

Photography

Where is there a camera shop?
Где фотомагазин?
gd'yeh fo-ta-ma-ga-ZEEN?

I need film
мне нужна плёнка
mn'yeh noozh-NA
   PL'YON-ka

for this camera
для этого фотоаппарата
dl'ya EH-ta-va fo-ta-ahp-
   pa-RA-ta

Black and white
чёрно-белая
CHOR-na-B'YEH-la-ya

Color film
цветная плёнка
tsv'yeht-NA-ya
   PL'YON-ka

Video film
видео плёнка
VEE-deh-yoh PL'YON-ka

battery
батарека
ba-ta-R'AY-ka

This is to be developed.
Это надо проявить.
EH-ta NA-da pra-ya-VEET.

How much per print?
Сколько стоит одно
   фото?
SKOHL'-ka STO-eet ahd-
   NO FO-toh?

Two prints of each.
Две копии каждой.
d'veh KO-pee
   KAHZH-doy.

Enlargement
увеличение
oo-veh-lee-
   CH'YEH-nee-yeh

About this size
такого размера
ta-KO-va rahz-MEH-ra

When will it be ready?
Когда будет готово?
kahg-DA BOO-d'yet ga-TOH-va?

May I take a picture of you?
Можно вас сфотографировать?
MO-zhna vahs sfa-ta-gra-FEE-ra-vaht?

Stand here, please.
Станьте здесь, пожа-
луйста.
*STAHN-t'yeh zd'yehs', pa-
ZHAHL'-sta.*

Don't move!
Не двигайтесь!
n'yeh D'VEE-guy-t'yehs'!

Smile!
Улыбка!
oo-LIP-ka!

That's it!
Вот так!
voht tahk!

May I send you a copy?
Можно вам послать копию?
MO-zhna vahm pa-SLAHT KO-pee-yoo?

Your name, please.
Ваше имя, пожалуйста.
*VA-sheh EE-m'ya, pa-
ZHAHL'-sta?*

Your address?
Ваш адрес?
vash AH-dress?

Can you take one of me?
Вы можете сфотографировать меня?
Vwee MO-zhe-t'yeh sfa-ta-gra-FEE-ra-vaht' m'yen-YA?

In front of this.
Перед этим.
PEH-reht EH-tim.

You are very kind.
Вы очень любезны.
*Vwee OH-chen'
l'yoo-B'YEZ-nee.*

Point to the Answer

In making arrangements in a фотомагазин (**fo-ta-ma-ga-ZEEN**), the following answers to questions should be useful. The sentence in Russian after the arrow asks the sales clerk to point to the answer.

> Укажите, пожалуйста, ваш ответ на мой вопрос на следующей странице. Большое спасибо.

Приходите завтра в _____ часа (в _____ часов).
Come back tomorrow at _____ o'clock.

Приходите через _____ дней (_____ дня).
Come back in _____ day. _____ days.

Мы можем исправить это.
We can repair it.

Мы не можем исправить это.
We cannot repair it.

У нас нет этого.
We don't have any.

Вы можете получить это в _____ .
You can get it at _____ .

13. Entertainment

Things to Do

May I invite you...
Можно Вас пригласить...
MO-zhna vahss pree-gla-SEET' ...

...to lunch?
...на обед?
...na AH-byet?

...to dinner?
...на ужин?
...na OO-zheen?

...for a drink?
...выпить?
...VWEE-peet'?

...to play chess?
...играть в шахматы?
...ee-GRAHT' f' SHAKH-ma-tee?

...to the theater?
...в театр?
...f'tee-AHTR?

...to the ballet?
...на балет?
...na ba-L'YET?

...to the movies?
...в кино?
...f' kee-NO?

...to play tennis?
...играть в теннис?
...ee-GRAHT f' TEN-nis?

May I ask you to dance?
Можно вас пригласить на танец?
MO-zhna vahss pree-gla-SEET na TA-nets?

Thank you very much!
Большое спасибо!
bahl'-SHO-yeh spa-SEE-ba!

With pleasure!
С удовольствием!
s' oo-da-VOL'ST-vee-yem!

Excuse me.
Извините.
eez-vee-NEE-t'yeh.

I cannot.
Я не могу.
ya n'yeh ma-GOO.

I am busy.
Я занят (m)
Я занята (f)
ya ZA-n'yaht (m)
ya ZA-n'ya-ta. (f)

I am tired.
Я устал (m)
Я устала (f)
ya oo-STAHL (m)
ya oo-STA-la (f)

I am waiting for someone.
Я жду одного человека.
ya zhdoo ad-na-VO che-la-V'YE-ka.

Where can we go tomorrow?
Куда мы можем пойти завтра?
koo-DA mwee MO-zhem pa'ee-TEE ZAHV-tra?

Let's go...
Пойдем...
pa-eed-YOM...

...to a restaurant.
...в ресторан.
...v' res-ta-RAHN.

. . . to a concert.
. . . на концерт.
. . . *na kohn-TSERT.*

. . . to the opera.
. . . в оперу.
. . . *v' OH-peh-roo.*

. . . to see national dances.
. . . смотреть национальные танцы.
. . . *sma-TRET' na-tsee-a-NAHL'-nee-yeh TAHN-tsee.*

. . . to a soccer game.
. . . на футбол.
. . . *na food-BOL.*

. . . to the art exhibit
. . . на выставку
. . . *na VWEE-stahf-koo*

. . . at the Hermitage (museum).
. . . в Эрмитаж
. . . *v' ehr-mee-TAHZH.*

Theaters and Nightclubs

Let's go to the theater.
Пойдём в театр.
paee-d'YOM f' tee-AHTR.

Two seats, please.
Два билета, пожалуйста.
dva-bee-L'YEH-ta, pa-ZHAHL'-sta.

Orchestra.
Партер.
pahr-TEHR.

Balcony.
Балкон.
bal-KOHN.

Are they good seats?
Это хорошие места?
EH-ta ha-RO-shee-yeh mes-TA?

When does it start?
Когда начинается?.
kahg-DA na-chee-NA-yet-s'ya?

Who is playing?
Кто играет?
ktoh ee-GRA-yet?

Who is dancing?
Кто танцует?
ktoh tahn-TSOO-yet?

She is wonderful!
Она прекрасна!
ah-NA pree-KRAHSS-na!

He dances excellently!
Он танцует отлично!
ohn tahn-TSOO-yet at-
LEECH-na!

How do you like it?
Как вам нравится?
kahk vahm N'RA-veet-sa?

It's very good!
Очень хорошо!
OH-chen' ha-ra-SHO!

It's great!
Замечательно!
za-meh-CHA-t'yel'-na!

It's very amusing!
Очень забавно.
OH-chen' za-BA-vna!

Is it already over?
Это уже закончилось?
EH-ta oo-ZHEH za-KOHN-chee-lahs?

Now let's go dance.
Теперь пойдем танцевать.
tee-p'yehr pa'ee-D'YOHM tahn-tseh-VAHT'.

A table near the dance floor, please.
Столик около танцплощадки, пожалуйста.
STO-lik OH-ka-la tahnts-pla-SHAHT-kee, pa-ZHAHL'-sta.

Shall we dance?
Пойдем танцевать?
paee-D'YOHM tahn-tseh-VAHT?

(Shall we stay) a little longer?
Ещё немножко?
yesh-CHO n'yeh-MNOHZH-ka?

(Don't) you think it's late?
Вы не думаете, уже поздно?
vwee n'yeh DOO-ma-yet-yeh, OO-ZHEH POHZ-dna?

No, it doesn't matter.
Нет, ничего.
n'yet', nee-cheh-VO.

An Invitation to Dinner

Can you come for dinner at our house?
Можете ли вы прийти на ужин к нам домой?
MO-zheh-t'yeh lee vwee pree-TEE na OO-zheen k'nahm da-MOY?

Monday at eight?
В понедельник в восемь?
f' pa-nee-D'YEL-neek v' VO-s'yem?

With great pleasure!
С удовольствием!
s' oo-da-VOHLST-v'yem!

If it's convenient for you.
Если вам это удобно.
YES-lee vahm ET-ta oo-DOHB-na.

Sorry I am late.
Извините, я опоздал. (m)
Извините, я опоздала. (f)
eez-vee-NEE-t'yeh, ya ah-pahz-DAL. (m)
eez-vee-NEE-t'yeh, ya ah-pahz-DA-la. (f)

Very glad to see you.
Очень рад (рада; рады) вас видеть.
Oh-chen' raht (fem., RA-da; pl., RA-dee)
 vahs VEED-yet'.

Make yourself at home!
Будьте как дома!
BOOD-t'yeh kahk DOH-ma!

What a beautiful house!
Какой красивый домБ
ka-KOY kra-SEE-vwee dohm!

Will you have something to drink?
Хотите что-нибудь выпить?
ha-TEET-yeh shtoh nee-BOOT VWEE-peet?

With pleasure!
С удовольствием!
s' oo-da-VOHL'ST-v'yem!

To your health!
За ваше здоровье!
za VA-sheh z'da-RO-v'yeh!

Dinner is on the table!
Ужин на столе!
OO-zheen na sta-L'YEH!

Will you sit here?
Садитесь сюда?
sa-DEE-t'yes' s'you-DA?

What a delicious meal!
Какая вкусная еда!
ka-KA-ya v'KOOS-na-ya yeh-DA!

Do have some more!
Возьмите ещё!
vahz'-MEET-yeh yesh-CHO!

Thank you, just a little.
Спасибо, немного.
spa-SEE-ba, n'yeh-M'NO-ga.

We had a wonderful time!
Мы провели прекрасное время!
mwee pro-v'yeh-LEE preh-KRAHSS-na-yeh VREM-ya!

I'm sorry, we must go.
Извините, мы должны идти.
eez-vee-NEET-yeh, mwee dahl-ZHNEE ee-TEE.

We are taking an early plane.
Мы садимся на ранний самолёт.
mwee sa-DEEM-s'ya na RA-nee sa-ma-L'YOT.

That's too bad!
Очень жаль!
O-chen' zhal'!

I'll take you to the hotel.
Я провожу вас до
  гостиницы.
*ya pra-va-ZHOO vahss da
  ga-STEE-neet-see.*

No, please don't bother!
Не беспокойтесь!
n'yeh b'yes-pa-KOY-t'yes'!

Many thanks
Большое спасибо
bahl-SHO-yeh spa-SEE-ba

for your hospitality!
за вашу
  гостеприимность!
*za VA-shoo ga-steh-
  PREEM-nohst'!*

You are welcome.
Не за что.
n'YEH za shtoh.

It was a pleasure.
Это было очень прият-
  но.
*EH-ta BWEE-la OH-chen'
  pree-YAHT-na.*

Come back soon!
Приходите снова!
*pree-kha-DEET-yeh
  SNO-va!*

All the best!
Всего хорошего!
*v'seh-VO kha-RO-
  sheeh-va!*

14. Talking to People

Most phrase books are to preoccupied with attending to one's wants and generally "getting along" to pay much attention to what you should say once you have met someone. The following expressions have been tested for everyday conversational frequency and, except for the rather special phrases at the end of the section, will be of immediate use for making conversation with anyone you meet.

Do you live in this city?
Вы живёте в этом городе?
vwee zheev-YO-t'yeh v EH-tahm GO-ra-d'yeh?

Where are you from?
Откуда вы?
oht-KOO-da vwee?

I am from St. Petersburg.
Я из Петербурга.
ya eez pee-t'yehr-BOOR-ga.

Is that so?
Действительно?
dayst-VEE-t'yel'-na?

It's a beautiful city.
Это очень красивый
   город.
*EH-ta OH-chen' kra-SEE-
   vwee GO-raht.*

I've been there.
Я был там. (m)
ya BWEEL tahm.

I would like to go there.
Я хотел бы поехать
   туда. (m)
*ya kha-t'YEL bwee pa-
   YEH-hat' too-DA.*

How long have you been here?
Как долго вы здесь?
kahk DOHL-ga vwee zd'yes?

I just arrived.
Я только прибыл.
ya TOHL'-ka PREE-beel.

How long will you be here?
Как долго вы будете здесь?
kahk DOHL-ga vwee BOOD-yet-yeh zd'yes?

I will be here one month.
Я буду здесь месяц.
ya BOO-doo zd'yes M'YEH-sits.

Where are you staying?
Где вы остановились?
*gd'yeh vwee ah-sta-na-
   VEE-l'eess?*

At what hotel?
В какой гостинице?
*f' ka-KOY
   ga-STEE-neet-seh?*

How do you like Moscow?
Как вам нравится Москва?
kahk vahm N'RA-veet-sa ma-SKVA?

Odessa?
Одесса?
ah-DEHS-sa?

Kiev?
Киев?
KEE-yef?

Very much!
Очень хорошо!
OH-chen ha-ra-SHO!

Very interesting!
Очень интересно!
OH-chen een-teer-YEHS-na!

Wonderful!
Прекрасно!
preh-KRAHSS-na!

Are you from Moscow?
Вы из Москвы?
vwee eez mahsk-VWEE?

No, I (am)...
Нет, я...
N'yet, ya...

from Belorussia.
из Белоруссии.
eez b'yeh-la-roo-SEE.

from the Baltic.
из Прибалтики.
eez pree-BAHL-tee-kee.

from Ukraine.
с Украины.
s' oo-kra-EE-nee.

from Siberia.
из Сибири.
eez see-BEE-ree.

from Armenia.
из Армении.
eez ahr-MEH-nee.

from Kazakstan.
из Казахстана.
eez ka-zahk-STA-na.

Have you ever been to America?
Вы были уже в Америке?
vwee BWEE-lee oo-ZHEN v'ah-MEH-ree-keh?

. . . to England?
в Англии?
v'AHN-glee?

Where did you go?
Куда вы ездили?
koo-DA vwee
YEZ-dee-lee?

Note: These examples of из (from) and в ("in" or "to")
are good examples of how the "cases" of words as used
in sentences change the spelling and pronunciation of a
word. See the explanation of cases on pages .

What do you think of. . .
Что вы думаете о. . .
shtoh vwee DOO-ma-yeh-
t'yeh oh. . .

American movies?
американских фильмах?
ah-meh-ree-KAHN-skih
FEEL-makh?

. . . American music?
. . . американской музыке?
. . . ah-meh-ree-KAHN-skoy MOO-zee-k'yeh?

. . . Russian music?
. . . русской музыке?
. . . ROOS-koy MOO-zee-
k'yeh?

. . . Russian dancing?
. . . русских танцах?
. . . ROOS-keeh
TAHN-tsahkh?

When people ask your opinion about something, you will
find the following comments helpful.

Fine!
Прекрасно!
preh-KRAS-na!

Beautiful!
Красиво!
kra-SEE-va!

Marvelous!
Чудесно
choo-D'YES-na!

Not bad.
Неплохо.
n'yeh-PLO-ha.

I have forgotten.
Я забыл (m).
ya za-BWEEL
(m).

Never.	**Sometimes.**	**I agree.**
Никогда.	Иногда.	Я согласен (m).
nee-kahg-DA.	*ee-nahg-DA.*	*ya sa-GLA-sen.* (m)

Often.	**Once.**	**Is it possible?**	**Of course.**
Часто.	Однажды.	Это возмож-	Конечно.
CHA-sta.	*ad-NAHZH-dee.*	но? *EH-ta vahz-MOZH-na?*	*ka-n'YETCH-na.*

I don't believe it.	**I think that...**	**I don't know...**
Я не верю.	Я думаю, что...	Я не знаю...
ya n'yeh-VEHR-yoo.	*ya DOO-ma-yoo sh'toh...*	*Ya n'yeh ZNA-yoo...*

Concerning relationships and professions...

Are you married?
Вы женаты? (m)
Вы замужем? (f)
vwee zheh-NA-tee? (m)
vwee ZA-moo-zhem? (f)

Do you have childen?
У вас есть дети?
oo vahss yest' D'YEH-tee?

Yes. I have.	**No. I don't have (any).**
Да. У меня есть.	Нет. У меня нет.
da. oo men-YA yest'.	*n'yet. oo men-YA n'yet.*

How many girls?
Сколько девочек?
*SKOHL'-ka
  D'YEH-va-chek?*

How many boys?
Сколько мальчиков?
*SKOHL'-ka
  MAHL'-chee-kahf?*

How old are they?	**...is he?**	**...is she?**
Сколько им лет?	...ему?	...ей?
SKOHL'-ka eem l'yet?	*...yeh-MOO?*	*...yay?*

My son is seven years old.
Моему сыну семь лет.
*ma-yeh-MOO SEE-noo
  S'YEM l'yet.*

My daughter is ten years old.
Моей дочери десять лет.
*ma-YEY DOH-cheh-ree
  D'YEH-s'yaht' l'yet.*

Here is a photograph.
Вот фотография.
voht fo-ta-GRA-fee-ya.

What attractive children!
Какие хорошенькие дети!
*Ka-KEE-yeh
  ha-RO-shen'-kee-yeh
  D'YEH-tee!*

This is my	**...mother.**	**...wife.**
Это моя	...мама.	...жена.
EH-tah ma-YA	*...MA-ma.*	*...zheh-NA.*

...sister.
...сестра.
...see-STRA.

...daughter.
...дочь.
...dohch.

This is my
Это мой
EH-ta moy

...**father.**
...отец.
...*ah-T'YETS.*

...**husband.**
...муж.
...*moozh.*

...**brother.**
...брат.
...*braht.*

...**son.**
...сын.
...*sin.*

Do you know that person?
Вы знаете этого человека?
vwee ZNA-yet'-yeh EH-ta-va cheh-la-V'YEH-ka?

What is his (her) name?
Как его (её) зовут?
kahk yeh-VO (yeh-YO) za-VOOT?

He is
Он
ohn

...**a writer.**
...писатель.
...*pee-SA-tel'.*

...**an artist.**
...художник.
...*hoo-DOHZH-neek.*

...**a businessman.**
...бизнесмен.
...*biz-ness-MEN.*

...**a lawyer.**
...юрист.
...*yoo-REEST.*

...**a doctor.**
...врач.
...*vrahtch.*

...**an actor.**
...артист.
...*ar-TEEST.*

...**a scientist.**
...учёный.
...*oo-CHYO-nee.*

...**an engineer.**
...инженер.
...*een-zheh-N'YER.*

Do you know that lady?	**She is**	**...an actress.**
Вы знаете эту женщину?	Она	... актриса.
Vwee ZNA-yet-yeh EH-too zhen-SHEE-noo?	*ah-NA*	*... ak-TREE-sa.*

...an architect.
... архитектор.
... ar-hee-T'YEHK-tor.

...teacher.
... учительница.
... oo-CHEE-t'yel'-neet-sa.

...a musician.
... музыкант.
... moo-zee-KAHNT.

...a dancer.
... танцовщица.
... tahn-TSOV-sh'chee-tsa.

15. Words That Show You Are "With It"

There are certain words that Russian-speaking people use constantly, which do not have an exact equivalent in English. To use them at the right time will indicate to Russian people that you have good manners and are familiar with the most frequently used Russian conversational phrases—in other words, that you are "with it." The Russian expressions are given first to make it easier for you to recognize them as they occur in everyday conversation.

We have divided these terms into two groups. The first is composed of selected polite expressions.

Наилучшие пожелания!
*na-ee-l'YOO-shee-yeh
pa-zheh-LA-nee-ya!*
Best wishes!

Удачи!
oo-DA-chee!
Good luck!

Счастливого пути!
*shas-TLEE-va-va
poo-TEE!*
A good trip!

Добро пожаловать!
da-BRO pa-ZHA-lo-vaht'!
Welcome (to a guest)

Всего хорошего!
fsyeh-VO ha-RO-sheh-va!
All the best!

Поздравляю!
pa-zdrav-L'YA-yoo!
I congratulate! (you)

Будьте здоровы!
*BOOD-t'yeh
  zda-RO-vwee!*
Be healthy! (also said
  after a sneeze)

˙Того же и вам!
ta-VO zheh ee vahm!
The same to you!

Приятного аппетита!
*pree-YAHT-na-va
  ah-peh-TEE-ta!*
Enjoy your food!

Вы очень добры.
*Vwee OH-chen'
  DOH-bree.*
You are very kind.

С удовольствием.
*s' oo-da-VOHL-
  st'vee-yem.*
With pleasure.

Здорово!
ZDO-ra-va!
Great!

Замечательно!
za-meh-CHA-t'yel-na!
Wonderful!

Because the following phrases permeate conversation, it
will interest you to know what they mean, as well as to
learn to use them as conversational stopgaps. The
translations are extremely free, since these expressions
are often very idiomatic.

Что случилось?
shtoh sloo-CHEE-lahs'?
What happened?

Что нового?
shtoh NO-va-va?
What's new?

Правда?
PRAHV-da?
Really?

Как дела?
kahk d'yel-LA?
How's it going?

Отлично!
aht-LEETCH-na!
Excellently!

Совсем нет.
saf-S'YEM n'yet.
Not at all.

Я сожалею.
ya sa-zha-l'YEH-yoo.
I am sorry.

Точно так же.
TOHCH-na TAHK-zhe.
Just the same way.

В чём дело?
f'chohm D'YEH-la?
What's going on?

Договорились!
da-ga-va-REE-lees'!
Agreed!

Пошли!
pahsh-LEE!
Let's go!

Конечно.
ka-N'YESH-na.
Naturally, of course.

Не так ли?
n'yeh tahk lee?
Isn't it so?

Затем...
za-T'YEM...
and then...

Невероятно!
n'yeh v'yeh-ra-YAHT-na!
Incredible!

Ужасно!
oo-ZHA-sna!
Terrible!

Ради Бога!
RAH-dee BO-ga!
For God's sake!

Слава Богу!
SLA-va BO-goo!
Glory to God!
(thank God!)

Пока!
Pa-KA!
So long!

And, for making a toast . . .

За ваше здоровье!
Za VA-sheh zda-RO-v'yeh!
To your health!

За дружбу!
za-DROOZH-boo!
To friendship!

За мир!
za MEER!
To peace!

16. Shopping

Names of Shops

Please tell me where there is a...
Скажите, пожалуйста, где...
*ska-ZHEE-t'yeh
pa-ZHAHL'-sta
g'd'yeh...*

...clothing shop.
...магазин одежды.
*ma-ga-ZEEN
ahd-YEZH-dee.*

for men.
для мужчин.
dl'ya moosh-CHEEN.

for women.
для женщин.
dl'ya ZHEN-sh'cheen.

a shoe store.
магазин обуви.
*ma-ga-ZEEN
OH-boo-vee.*

a jewelry shop.
ювелирный магазин.
*yoo-veh-LEER-nee
ma-ga-ZEEN.*

a pharmacy.
аптека.
ahp-T'YEH-ka.

a bookstore.
книжный магазин.
*K'NEEZH-nee
ma-ga-ZEEN.*

a grocery store.
продуктовый магазин.
*pra-dook-TOH-vee
ma-ga-ZEEN.*

a market.
рынок.
REE-nok.

a barber shop.
парикмахерская.
pa-reek-MA-hair-ska-ya.

a beauty shop.
дамская
парикмахерская.
*DAHM-ska-ya
pa-reek-MA-hair-
ska-ya.*

a toy shop.
магазин игрушек.
*ma-ga-ZEEN
ee-GROO-shek.*

a flower shop.
цветочный магазин.
*tsveh-TOHCH-nee
ma-ga-ZEEN.*

an antique shop.
антикварный магазин.
*ahn-teek-VAR-nee
ma-ga-ZEEN.*

a bakery.
булочная.
BOO-latch-na-ya.

General Shopping Vocabulary

What do you wish?
Что вы желаете?
*shtoh vwee zhe-LA-ye-t'y-
eh?*

I'm just looking.
Я просто смотрю.
ya PRO-sta sma-TR'YEW.

I'll be back later.
Я вернусь позже.
ya v'yehr-NOOS' POZH-zheh.

I would like something...
Я хотел бы что-нибудь...
ya kha-T'YEL-bwee SHTOH-nee-boot'...

for my husband.
для моего мужа.
dl'ya ma-yeh-VOH MOO-zha.

for my wife.
для моей жены.
dl'ya ma-YAY zeeh-NEE.

for myself.
для себя.
dl'ya sehb-YA.

for a man.
для мужчины.
dl'ya moosh-CHEEN-ee.

for a woman.
для женщины.
dl'ya ZHEN-sh'chee-nee.

I like this... that.
Мне нравится это... то.
mn'yeh NRA-veet-sya EH-ta... toh.

How much is it?
Сколько это стоит?
SKOHL'-ka EH-ta STO-eet?

Show me another.
Покажите мне другое.
pa-ka-ZHEET-yeh mn'yeh droo-GOY-yeh.

Not so expensive.
Не так дорого.
n'yeh tahk DO-ra-ga.

How do you like this?
Как вам нравится это?
kahk vahm NRA-veet-sa EH-ta?

May I try it on?
Можно примерить?
MOHZH-na pree-M'YEH-reet'?

That suits you very well.
Это вам очень идёт.
EH-ta vahm OH-chen' eed-YOHT.

Can you alter it?
Можете вы переделать это?
MO-zheh-t'yeh vwee peh-reh-d'YEL-laht' EH-ta?

Good! I'll take it.
Хорошо! Я беру.
ha-ra-SHO! ya b'yeh-ROO.

Is this handmade?
Это ручная работа?
EH-ta rooch-NA-ya ra-BO-ta?

Is this hand embroidered?
Это ручная вышивка?
EH-ta rooch-NA-ya VEE-sheev-ka?

Can you send it...
Можно это послать...
MOHZH-na EH-ta pa-SLAHT'...

to this hotel?
в эту гостиницу?
v' EH-too ga-STEE-nee-tsoo?

A receipt, please.
Квитанция, пожалуйста.
qvee-TAHN-tsee-ya, pa-ZHAHL'-sta.

Some small change.
Несколько монет.
N'YEH-skahl'-ka ma-N'YEHT.

The change, please.
Сдача, пожалуйста.
ZDA-cha, pa ZHAHL'-sta.

Point to the Answer

Укажите, пожалуйста, ваш ответ на мой вопрос на следующей странице. Большое спасибо.

We haven't any.
У нас нет.
oo nahs n'yet.

We have nothing larger.
У нас нет ничего побольше.
oo nahs n'yeht nee-cheh-VOH pa-BOHL'-sheh.

Nothing smaller.
Ничего поменьше.
nee-cheh-VO pa-M'YEHN'-sheh.

We don't deliver.
Мы не доставляем на дом.
mwee n'yeh dahs-tahv-L'YAH-yehm NA-dahm.

We can't ship it to America.
Мы не посылаем это в Америку.
mwee n'yeh pa-see-LA-yehm EH-ta v ah-MEH-ree-koo.

We can't accept personal checks.
Мы не принимаем персональные чеки.
mwee n'yeh pree-nee-MA-yehm pehr-sa-NAHL'-nee-yeh CHEH-kee.

Come back again!
Приходите снова!
pree-ha-DEE-t'yeh SNO-va!

Clothes

Blouse	**Suit**	**Shirt**	**Dress**
блуза	костюм	рубашка	платье
BLOO-za	*ka-ST'YOOM*	*roo-BA-shka*	*PLA-t'yeh*

fur hat	**scarf**	**handbag**	**gloves**
меховая	шарф	сумочка	перчатки
шапка	*sharf*	*SOO-*	*pehr-CHANT-*
m'yeh-		*mahtch-ka*	*kee*
ha-VA-ya			
SHAHP-ka			

Shoes	**boots**	**boots (snow)**
туфли	сапоги	валенки
TOOF-lee	*sa-pa-GHEE*	*VA-len-kee*

stockings	**socks**
чулки	носки
chool-KEE	*nahs-KEE*

brassiere	**panties**
лифчик	трусы
LEEF-cheek	*troo-SEE*

pants	**skirt**
брюки	юбка
BR'YOO-kee	*YOOP-ka*

jacket	sweater	necktie
пиджак	свитер	галстук
peed-ZHAK	*SVEE-ter*	*GAL-stook*

underwear	pajamas
нижнее бельё	пижама
NEEZH-neh-yeh b'yel'YO	*pee-ZHA-ma*

Russian blouse	fur coat	fur hat
народная	шуба	меховая шапка
рубашка	*SHOO-ba*	*m'yeh-ha-VA-ya*
na-ROHD-na-ya		*SHAHP-ka*
roo-BA-shka		

umbrella	raincoat	swimsuit (m)	swimsuit (w)
зонтик	плащ	плавки	купальник
ZOHN-teek	*plahsh'CH*	*PLAHF-kee*	*koo-PAHL'-neek*

Sizes—Colors—Materials

What size?	small
какой размер?	маленький
ka-KOY rahz- M'YER?	*MA-l'yen'-kee*

medium	large
средний	большой
SR'YED-nee	*bahl-SHOY*

larger	smaller	wider
побольше	поменьше	шире
pa-BOHL'-sh'yeh	*pa-M'YEHN'-sheh*	*SHEE-r'yeh*

narrower	**longer**	**shorter**
у́же	длиннее	короче
OO-zheh	*d'lee-N'YEH-yeh*	*ka-RO-cheh*

What color?	**red**	**yellow**	**blue**
какого цвета?	красный	жёлтый	синий
ka-KO-va TSV'YE-ta?	*KRA-snee*	*ZHOHL-tee*	*SEE-n'ee*

green	**brown**	**pink**
зелёный	коричневый	розовый
zeh-L'YO-nee	*ka-REECH-n'yeh-vwee*	*RO-za-vwee*

gray	**black**	**white**
серый	чёрный	белый
S'YEH-ree	*CHOR-nee*	*B'YEH-lee*

Is it silk?	**linen**	**velvet**	**wool**
Это шёлк?	лён	бархат	шерсть
EH-ta sholk?	*l'yon*	*BAR-hat*	*sherst'*

cotton	**lace**	**synthetic**
хлопок	кружева	синтетика
KHLO-pohk	*kroo-zheh-VA*	*seen-TEH-tee-ka*

leather	**kid**	**plastic**
кожа	лайка	пластик
KO-zha	*LAI-ka*	*pla-STEEK*

What fur is this?	fox	seal
Что это за мех?	лиса	нерпа
shtoh EH-ta za m'yekh?	*lee-SA*	*NEHR-pa*

mink	sable	rabbit
норка	соболь	кролик
NOR-ka	*SO-bahl*	*KRO-leek*

Newsstand

I need (a)...	map of the city	postcards
Мне нужно...	план города	открытки
mn'yeh NOO-zhna...	*plahn GO-ra-da*	*aht-KREET-kee*

Have you a newspaper in English?
У вас есть газета по-английски?
oo vahs yest' ga-Z'YEH-ta pa-ahn-GLEE-skee?

in French?	in German?
по-французски?	по-немецки?
pa-fran-TSOO-skee?	*pa-nee-M'YET-skee?*

Tobacco Shop

Have you American cigarettes?
Есть ли у вас американские сигареты?
yest' lee oo vahs ah-meh-ree-KAHN-skee-yeh see-gah-R'YEH-tee?

No, but try	Russian cigarettes.
Нет, но попробуйте	русские сигареты.
n'yeht, noh pahp-ROH-booy-t'yeh	*ROOS-kee-yeh see-ga-R'YEH-tee.*

pipe	tobacco	cigar	matches
трубка	табак	сигара	спички
TROOP-ka	*ta-BAHK*	*see-GA-ra*	*SPEECH-kee*

Drugstore

Where is there a drugstore?
Где аптека?
gd'yeh ap-T'YEH-ka?

toothbrush	toothpaste
зубная щётка	зубная паста
zoob-NA-ya SH'CHOT-ka	*zoob-NA-ya PA-sta*

razor	razor blades	shaving cream
бритва	лезвие для бритья	крем для бритья
BREET-va	*LEZ-vee-yeh dl'ya bree-T'YA*	*KREM dl'ya bree-T'YA*

hairbrush	comb	scissors
щётка	гребешок	ножницы
SH'CHOT-ka	*greh-b'yeh-SHOHK*	*NOHZH-nee-tsee*

iodine	aspirin	vitamin pills
йод	аспирин	витамины
yohd	*ah-spee-REEN*	*vee-ta-MEE-nee*

antiseptik
антисептик
an-tee-SEP-teek

eye drops
глазные капли
*glahz-NEE-yeh
KAHP-lee*

nail polish
лак для ногтей
*LAHK dl'yah
nahk-T'YEY*

cough medicine
лекарство от
кашля
*l'yeh-KAHR-stva
oht KAHSH-
l'ya*

sunglasses
тёмные очки
*T'YOHM-nee-yeh
atch-KEE*

shampoo
шампунь
sham-POON'

Cosmetics

powder
пудра
POO-dra

lipstick
губная помада
*goob-NA-ya
pa-MA-da*

mascara
тушь
TOOSH

eye shadow
тени
T'YEH-nee

eyebrow pencil
карандаш для бровей
*ka-rahn-DAHSH dl'ya
bro-V'YEY*

hairspray
лак для волос
*lahk dl'ya va-
LOHS*

hair pins
шпильки
SHPEEL'-kee

perfume
духи
doo-HEE

Beauty Parlor

Shampoo, please
Помыть волосы,
   пожалуйста.
pa-MWEET' VOH-la-see,
   pa-ZHAHL'-sta.

Tint it, please.
Покрасить, пожалуйста.
pahk-RA-seet,
   pa-ZHAHl'-sta.

The same color.
Тот же самый
   цвет.
toht zhe SA-
   mwee tsv'yet

lighter
светлее
sv'yeht-L'YEH-
   yeh

darker
темнее
t'yehm-N'YEH-
   yeh

manicure
маникюр
ma-nee-K'YOOR

pedicure
педикюр
peh-dee-K'YOOR

Barber

shave
брить
breet'

haircut
стрижка
STREEZH-ka

massage
массаж
ma-SAHZH

Scissors, please.
Ножницы,
   пожалуйста.
NOHZH-nee'-
   tsee, pa-
   ZHAHL'-sta.

shorter
короче
ka-ROH-cheh

not too much
не слишком
n'yeh-
   SLEESH-kahm.

on top	in back	this side
на макушке	сзади	эта сторона
na ma-KOOSH-k'yeh	*S'ZA-dee*	*EH-ta sta-ra-NA*

the other side	That's fine!
другая сторона	Отлично!
droo-GA-ya sta-ra-NA	*aht-LEECH-na!*

Food Market

I need...	this	that
Мне нужно...	это	то
mn'yeh NOOZH-na...	*EH-tah*	*toh*

What is this?	Is this fresh?
Что это?	Это свежие?
shtoh EH-tah?	*EH-ta SVEH-zhee?*

How much per kilo?	Two kilos.
Сколько стоит кило?	Два кило.
SKOHL'-ka STOH-eet kee-LO?	*dva kee-LO.*

Caviar—three jars.	Vodka—two bottles.
Икра—три банки.	Водка—две бутылки.
eek-RA—tree BAHN-kee.	*VOD-ka—dv'yeh boo-TEEL-kee.*

In a bag, please.
В сумке, пожалуйста.
f' SOOM-keh, pa-ZHAHL'-sta.

Jewelry

How much is...   **this watch?**   **this ring?**
Сколько   эти часы?   это кольцо?
    стоит...   *EH-tee cha-SEE?*   *EH-ta*
SKOHL'-ka   *kahl'-TSOH?*
    STO-eet...

this bracelet?   **this necklace?**
этот браслет?   это ожерелье?
EH-taht bra-SLET?   *EH-ta ah-zheh-*
                                     R'YEH-l'yeh?

these earrings?   **Is this gold?**   **silver?**
эти серёжки?   Это золото?   серебро?
EH-tih seh-   *EH-ta*   *s'yeh-r'yeh-BRO?*
    R'YEZH-kee?   *zo-la-TOH?*

platinum   **silver plated**   **gold plated**
платина   посеребренное   позолоченное
PLA-tee-na   *pa-s'yeh-r'yeh-*   *pa-za-LOH-*
                 BR'YOH-   *ch'yeh-na-yeh*
                 no-yeh

Are these real or   **diamond**   **ruby**
    imitation?   бриллиант   рубин
Это настоящий   *breel-YAHNT*   *roo-BEEN*
    или имита-
    ция?
EH-tah na-sta-
    YA-shee EE-lee
    ee-mee-TA-
    tsee-yah?

emerald	saphire	pearl
изумруд	сапфир	жемчуг
ee-zoom-ROOT	*sahp-FEER*	*ZHEHM-chook*

They are very expensive, aren't they?
Они очень дорогие, не так ли?
ah-NEE OH-chen' da-ra-GHEE-yeh, n'yeh tahk lee?

Antiques

How old is this?
Сколько этому лет?
*SKOHL'-ka EH-ta-moo
l'yet?*

How much is...
Сколько стоит...
SKOHL'-ka STO-eet...

...this book?
...эта книга?
*...EH-ta
KNEE-ga*

**...this pain-
ting?**
...эта картина?
*...EH-ta
kar-TEE-na?*

...this box?
...эта шкатул-
ка?
*...EH-ta shka-
TOOL-ka?*

...this rug?
...этот ковёр?
...EH-toht ka-V'YOR?

...this icon?
...эта икона?
...EH-ta ee-KO-na?

It's beautiful!
Это красиво!
EH-ta kra-SEE-va!

17. Telephone

Where is the telephone?
Где телефон?
g'd'yeh teh-leh-FOHN?

Hello!
Алло!
ah-LO!

Please, the telephone number of _____ .
Пожалуйста, номер телефона _____ .
pa-ZHAHL'-sta, NO-mer teh-leh-FO-na _____ .

Please, connect me with number _____ in Moscow.
Пожалуйста, соедините меня с номером
_____ в Москве.
pa-ZHAHL'-sta, sa-yeh-dee-NEE-t'yeh meen-YA s NO-meh-ram _____ v' mohsk-VEH.

Information.
Информация.
een-for-MAHT-s'ya.

Long distance.
Междугородний.
mezh-doo-ga-RO-d'nee.

I want the Hotel Pulkovskaya
Мне нужна гостиница Пулковская
mn'yeh noozh-NA ga-STEE-nee-tsa POOL-kov-ska-ya

in St. Petersburg.
в Петербурге
f' pee-t'yehr-BOORG-'yeh.

(Extension) number at the hotel _____ .
Номер в гостинице _____ .
NO-mer v' ga-STEE-nee-tse _____ .

How long must I wait?
Как долго я должен ждать?
kahk DOHL-ga ya DOHL-zhen zhdaht'?

How much per minute?
Сколько стоит одна минута?
SKOHL'ka STO-eet ahd-NA mee-NOO-ta?

This is Valentin Markov speaking.
Это говорит Валентин Марков.
EH-ta ga-va-REET va-len-TEEN MAR-kohf.

May I speak with Ivan?
Можно говорить с
    Иваном?
*MO-zhna ga-va-REET'
    s'ee-VA-nom?*

...with Marina?
...с Мариной?
...s' ma-REE-noy?

He (she) isn't here.
Его (её) нет.
yeh-VO (yeh-YO) n'yeht.

Please call back.
Перезвоните,
    пожалуйста.
*p'yeh-r'yez-vo-NEE-t'yeh,
    pa-ZHAHL'-sta.*

Hold the line.
Подождите.
pa-dahzh-DEE-t'yeh.

When is he (she) coming back?
Когда он (она) вернётся?
kahg-DA ohn (ah-NA) vehr-N'YOT-s'ya?

Thank you.
Спасибо.
spa-SEE-ba.

I'll call again.
Я позвоню снова.
ya pa-zva-n'YOO SNO-va.

Can you take a message for him (her)?
Вы можете передать ему (ей)?
vwee MO-zhet-yeh peh-r'yeh-DAHT' yeh-MOO (yey)?

Ask him (her) to call me.
Попросите его (ее) мне позвонить.
pa-pra-SEE-t'yeh yeh-VO (yeh-YOH) mn'yeh pahz-va-NEET'.

My number is...
Мой номер...
moy NO-mer...

My name is...
Меня зовут...
men-YA za-VOOT...

I'll spell my first name:
Я продиктую моё имя:
ya pra-dek-TOO-yoo ma-YO EEM-ya:

...middle name
...отчество
...OHT-chest-va

...family name
...фамилия
...fa-MEE-lee-ya

THE CYRILLIC ALPHABET

RUSSIAN LETTER	PRONUNCIATION OF THE NAMES OF THE RUSSIAN LETTERS	EQUIVALENT IN ENGLISH LETTERS OR LETTER COMBINATIONS
А	*ah*	a
Б (б)	*bay*	b (or p at end of word)
В(в)	*vay*	v (or f at end of word)
Г	*gay*	g (or k at end of word)
Д	*day*	d (or t at end of word)
Е	*yay*	yeh
Ё	*yo*	yo
Ж	*zhay*	zh
З	*zay*	z
И	*ee*	e
Й	*ee KRAHT-ko-yeh*	oy
К	*kha*	k
Л	*el*	l
М	*em*	m
Н	*en*	n
О	*oh*	o
П	*pay*	p
Р	*er*	r
С	*es*	s
Т	*tay*	t
У	*oo*	u
Ф	*ef*	f
Х	*kha*	h (guttural)
Ц	*tseh*	ts
Ч	*cheh*	ch
Ш	*sha*	sh
Щ	*sh'cha*	sh'ch
Ъ	*(tv'YOR-dee znahk)*	(indicates an apostrophe, ending to word or syllable)

Ы		ee (very open)
		(like the *i* in "sit")
Ь	*(m'YA-kee znahk)*	(indicates a "soft" ending
		to word or syllable)
Э	*eh (oh-bo-ROHT-no-yeh)*	eh
Ю	*yoo*	yu
Я	*ya*	ya

Where is a public phone?
Где телефон-автомат?
gd'yeh t'yel-leh-FOHN ahf-tah-MAHT?

What is the information number?
Какой номер справочнкого бюро?
ka-KOY NO-mer SPRA-vahch-na-va byou-ROH?

Can you change a ruble?
Вы можете разменять рубль?
vwee MO-zheh-t'yeh rahz-men-YAHT' roobl'?

What coin do I put in?
Какую монету нужно опустить?
*kah-KOO-yoo ma-N'YE-too NOOZH-na
ah-poo-STEET'?*

And, if there is no public telephone available:

May I use your phone?
Можно позвонить от вас?
MO-zhna paz-va-NEET' aht VAHS?

Certainly.
Конечно.
kahn-YESH-na.

How much do I owe you?
Сколько я вам должен?
SKOHL'-ka ya vahm DOHL-zhen?

Nothing.
Ничего.
nee-cheh-VO.

You are very kind.
Вы очень любезны.
vwee OH-chen' l'yoo-B'YEZ-nee.

Thank you.
Спасибо.
spa-SEE-ba.

Hello! Operator!
Алло! Телефонистка!
ahl-lo! teh-leh-fa-NIST-ka!

That was a wrong number.
Вы не туда попали.
vwee n'ye too-DAH pah-PAH-lee.

Please try again.
Перезвоните, пожалуйста.
p'yeh-rez-va-NEE-t'yeh, pa-ZHAHL'-sta.

18. Post Office

Where is the post office?
Где почта?
g'd'yeh POHCH-ta?

...a mail box?
...почтовый ящик?
*...pach-THO-vwee
YA-sh'cheek?*

Stamps for five letters.
Марки для пяти писем.
*MAR-kee dl'ya p'ya-TEE
PEE-sem.*

Express mail.
Экспрессом.
eks-PRES-sam.

How much is needed?
Сколько нужно?
SKOHL'-ka NOOZH-na?

For a letter to the USA?*
Для письма в США?
dl'ya pees'-MA f' SEH-SHEH-AH?

...to Canada?
...в Канаду?
...f' ka-NA-doo?

...to Spain?
...в Испанию?
...v' ees-PA-nee-yoo?

...to Germany?
...в Германию?
...*v' gher-MA-nee-yoo?*

...to France?
...во Францию?
...*vah FRAHN-tsee-yoo?*

...to England?
...в Англию?
...*v' AHN-glee-yoo?*

...to Australia?
...в Австралию?
...*v' ahf-STRA-lee-yoo?*

...to Greece?
...в Грецию?
...*v' GREH-tsee-yoo?*

...to Austria?
...в Австрию?
...*v' AHF-stree-yoo?*

* For names of other countries, see dictionary. Note that
в meaning "to" requires the **accusative** form for the
destination, which in the feminine singular is often Ю
(names of countries are generally feminine). See
grammatical table on pages 133–139.

Where can I send a telegram?
Где можно послать телеграмму?
gd'yeh MO-zhna pa-SLAHT' teh-leh-GRA-moo?

...a telex?
...телекс?
...*TEH-leks?*

...a fax?
...факс?
...*fahx?*

I need writing paper.
Мне нужна бумага.
*m'n'yeh noozh-NA
   boo-MA-ga.*

...envelopes.
...конверты.
...*kahn-VER-tee.*

...a pen.
...ручка.
...*ROOCH-ka.*

...a pencil.
...карандаш.
...*ka-rahn-DAHSH.*

A short letter:

Dear Vladimir,
Дорогой Владимир,
da-ro-GOY vla-DEE-meer,

Dear Katya,
Дорогая Катя,
da-ra-GA-ya KAHT-ya,

Best regards from St. Petersburg.
Привет из Петербурга.
preev-YET eez pee-t'yehr-BOOR-ga.

This city is beautiful!
Это очень красивый город!
EH-ta OH-chen' kra-SEE-vwee GO-raht!

I am enjoying this trip very much!
Это путешествие мне нравится!
EH-ta poo-tee-SHE-vee-yeh mn'yeh NRA-vee-tsa!

I miss you.
Я скучаю по тебе.
ya skoo-CHA-yoo pa t'yeh-B'YEH.

Best wishes to everyone!
Наилучшие пожелания всем!
nai-LOOCH-shee-yeh pa-zheh-LA-nee-ya f' s'yem!

Sincerely,
Искренне,
EESK-ren-n'yeh,

With love!
С любовью!
s' l'yoo-BO-v'yoo!

— Катя (Katya)

— Владимир (Vladimir)

19. Seasons and Weather

Winter	Spring	Summer	Autumn
зима	весна	лето	осень
zee-MA	*ves-NA*	*L'YEH-ta*	*OH-sen'*

How is the weather today?
Какая сегодня погода?
ka-KA-ya seh-VO-dn'ya pa-GO-da?

The weather is fine.
Погода хорошая.
pa-GO-da ha-RO-sha-ya.

It is raining.
Идёт дождь.
eed-YOHT dohsht'.

It is snowing.
Идёт снег.
eed-YOHT snek.

It is freezing.
Гололед.
ga-la-L'YOHT.

I am very cold.
Мне очень холодно.
mn'yeh oh-chen' HO-lad-na.

I need an umbrella.	**...a raincoat.**	**...boots.**
Мне нужен зонтик.	...плащ.	...сапоги.
mn'yeh NOO-zhen ZOHN-teek.	*...plahsh'ch.*	*...sa-pa-GHEE.*

Do you like to ski?	**...to ice skate?**
Вы любите кататься на лыжах?	...кататься на коньках?
vwee L'YOO-beet-yah ka-TA-tsa na LEE-zhakh?	*...ka-TA-Tsa na kahn'-KAHKH?*

When does the thaw come?
Когда будет оттепель?
KAHG-da BOOD-yet OH-teh-p'yel'?

Now it is very hot.	**Let's go swimming.**
Сейчас очень жарко.	Пойдём плавать.
say-CHAHS OH-chen' ZHAR-ka.	*pa-ee-D'YOHM PLA-vaht'.*

Where is the pool?	**...the beach?**
Где бассейн?	...пляж?
gd'yeh ba-SAYN?	*...pl'yahzh?*

I want to rent a boat.
Я хочу взять лодку.
ya kha-CHOO vz'yaht' LOHT-koo.

. . .a mask and fins.
. . .маску и ласты.
. . .*MA-skoo ee LA-stee.*

Is it safe to swim here?
Безопасно ли плавать здесь?
b'yeh-za-PAHS-na lee PLA-vaht' zd'yes?

20. Doctor and Dentist

I am ill.
Я болен.
ya BOH-l'yehn.

He is ill.
Он болен.
ohn BOH-l'yen.

She is ill.
Она больна.
ah-NA bohl'-NA.

We need a doctor.
Нам нужен врач.
nahm NOO-zhen vrahch.

When can the doctor come?
Когда может прийти врач?
kahg-DA MO-zhet pree-TEE vrahch?

What is wrong with you?
Что с вами!
shtoh s VA-mee?

Where does it hurt?
Где болит?
gd'yeh ba-LEET?

Here.
Здесь.
zd'yes'.

I have a pain
У меня болит
oo m'yen-YA ba-LEET

...(in) the head.
...голова.
...ga-la-VA.

He (she) has a pain...
У него (неё) болит...
oo n'yeh-VO (n'yeh-YO)
  ba-LEET...

...the throat.
...горло.
...GOR-la.

...the ear.
...ухо.
...OO-ha.

...the stomach.
...живот.
...zhee-VOHT.

...the back.
...спина.
...spee-NA.

...the leg.
...нога.
...na-GA.

...the arm.
...рука.
...roo-KA.

...the hand.
...кисть.
...keest'.

...the foot.
...ступня.
...stoop-N'YA.

I feel dizzy.
У меня кружится
  голова.
oo m'yen-YA KROO-zheet-
  s'ya ga-la-VA.

I have a fever.
У меня температура.
oo m'yen-YA tem-peh-ra-
  TOO-ra.

I cannot sleep.
Я не могу спать.
ya n'yeh ma-GOO spaht'.

I have diarrhea.
У меня понос.
oo m'yen-YA pa-NOSS.

Since when?
Как давно?
kahk dav-NO?

Since yesterday.
С вчера.
s' f'cheh-RA.

For three days.
Три дня.
tree dn'ya.

What are you eating?
Что вы едите?
shtoh vee yeh-DEE-t'yeh?

Undress.
Разденьтесь.
raz-D'YEN'-t'yes'.

Lie down.
Ложитесь.
la-ZHEE-t'yes'.

Open (your) mouth.
Откройте рот.
aht-KROY-t'yeh roht.

Show me your tongue.
Покажите мне язык.
pa-ka-ZHEE-t'yeh mn'yeh ya-ZEEK.

Sit up.
Сядьте.
S'YAHT-t'yeh.

Cough!
Покашляйте!
pa-KASH-l'yai-t'yeh!

Breathe deeply!
Дышите глубоко!
dee-SHEE-t'yeh gloo-ba-KO!

Get dressed.
Оденьтесь.
ah-D'YEN'-t'yes'

Take this medicine.
Примите это лекарство.
pree-MEET-yeh EH-ta l'yeh-KARST-va.

. . .these pills.
. . .эти таблетки.
. . .EH-tee ta-BL'YET-kee.

Three times a day.
Три раза в день.
tree RA-za v' d'yen'.

You must stay in bed.
Вы должны лежать в постели.
vwee dahl-ZHNEE l'yeh-ZHAT' v' pa-STEH-lee.

Two days.
Два дня.
dva dn'ya.

Is it necessary to go to a hospital?
Нужно ли ехать в больницу?
NOOZH-na lee YEH-hat' v' bahl-NEET-soo?

Not now.
Не сейчас.
n'yeh sey-CHAHS.

Is it serious?
Это серьёзно?
EH-ta seh-R'YOZ-na?

No. It is not serious.
Нет. Это не серьёзно.
n'yet. EH-ta n'yeh seh-R'YOZ-na.

Don't worry.
Не беспокойтесь.
n'yeh b'yes-pa-KOY-t'yes'.

You have...
У вас...
oo vahss...

...indigestion.
...расстройство.
...ra-STROYST-va.

...an infection.
...инфекция.
...een-FEK-tsee-ya.

...a cold.
...простуда.
...pra-STOO-da.

I don't feel well.
Мне плохо.
mn'yeh PLO-ha.

Be careful.
Будьте осторожны.
BOOT-t'yeh ah-sta-ROHZH-nee.

Don't eat too much.
Не ешьте много.
n'yeh YESH-t'yeh MNO-ga.

Don't drink alcohol.
Не пейте алкоголь.
n'yeh PAY-t'yeh al-ka-
GOHL'.

How do you feel today?
Как вы чувствуете себя
сегодня?
kahk vwee CHOOST-voo-
yeh-t'yeh seb-YA
seh-VOHD-n'ya?

Sick.
болен.
BO-l'yen.

Better.
Лучше.
LOOT-sheh.

Much better.
Много лучше.
MNO-ga
LOOT-sheh.

Dentist

I need a dentist.
Мне нужен зубной врач.
m'n'yeh NOO-zhen zoob-
NOY vrahtch.

I have a toothache.
Я меня болит зуб.
oo men-YA ba-LEET zoop.

It hurts here.
Болит здесь.
ba-LEET zd'yes'.

Do I need a new filling?
Мне нужна новая пломба?
m'n'yeh noozh-NA NO-va-ya PLOHM-ba?

Can you fix it temporarily?
Вы можете сделать временно?
vwee MO-zhet-yeh ZD'YE-laht VREH-men-no?

I must extract this tooth.
Я должен вырвать этот зуб.
ya DOHL-zhen VWEER-vaht' EH-taht zoop.

How long will it take?
Как долго это будет?
*kahk DOHL-ga EH-ta
BOOD-yet?*

A few minutes.
Несколько минут.
*N'YEH-skohl'-ka
mee-NOOT.*

**Please,
novocaine.**
Пожалуйста,
новокаин.
*pa-ZHAHL'-sta,
no-va-ka-EEN.*

One moment!
Один момент!
*ah-DEEN
ma-MENT!*

Stop!
Постойте!
pa-STOY-t'yeh!

Does it still hurt?
Болит?
ba-LEET?

Yes, a little.
Да, немного.
da, n'yeh-MNO-ga.

No. Not at all.
Нет. Совсем не
болит.
*n'yet. sahf-
S'YEM n'yeh
ba-LEET.*

Is that all?
Это всё?
EH-ta vs'yo?

Yes, it's over.
Да, закончили.
*da, za-KOHN-
chee-lee.*

The bill, please.
Счёт, пожалуйста.
shch'yot, pa-ZHAHL'-sta.

And the receipt.
И квитанию.
kvee-TAHN-tsee-yoo.

21. Problems and Police

Go away!
Уходите!
oo-ha-DEE-t'yeh!

Or I'll call the police!
Или я позову милицию!
EE-lee ya pa-za-VOO mee-LEET-see-yoo!

Police!
Милиция!
mee-LEE-tsee-ya!

Help!
Помогите!
pa-ma-GHEE-t'yeh!

What's going on?
В чем дело?
f' chyom D'YEH-lo?

This man is annoying me!
Этот человек пристаёт ко мне!
EH-taht cheh-la-V'YEK pree-sta-YOT ka mn'yeh!

Where is the police station?
Где отделение милиции?
g'd'yeh aht-d'yeh-L'YEH-nee-ya mee-LEET-see-ee?

I have been robbed.
Меня ограбили.
men-YA ah-GRA-bee-lee.

My watch is missing.
У меня пропали часы.
oo m'ye-N'YA pra-PAH-lee cha-SEE.

My wallet...
бумажник...
boo-MAHZH-neek...

My jewelry...
драгоцен-ности...
dra-ga-TSEN-na-stee...

I've lost my passport.
Я потерял паспорт.
ya pa-ter-YAHL PA-sport.

...suitcase.
...чемодан.
...cheh-ma-DAHN.

Stop!
Стой!
stoy!

That's the man!
Вот этот человек!
voht EH-tat cheh-la-VEK!

There he is!
Вот он!
voht ohn!

This one?
Этот?
EH-taht?

Are you certain?
Вы уверены?
vwee oo-VEH-reh-nee?

I don't recognize him.
Я не узнаю его.
ya n'yeh ooz-na-YOO yeh-VO.

Notify the American Consulate.
Сообщите в американское консульство.
sa-ap-SHCH'EE-t'ye v' ah-meh-ree-KAHN-ska-yeh
  KOHN- sool'st-va.

Wait! The hotel found your things.
Подождите! В гостинице нашлись ваши вещи.
pa-dazh-DEE-t'yeh! v' ga-STEE-nee-tseh nahsh-LEESS
  VA-shee VESH-chee.

It's a mistake.	**Don't worry.**
Это ошибка.	Не беспокойтесь.
EH-ta ah-SHEEP-ka.	*n'yeh b'yes-pa-KOY-*
	t'yes'.

May I go now?
Ш могу идти?
ya ma-GOO eed-TEE?

22. Some Business Phrases

You will find the short phrases and vocabulary in this
section extremely useful if you are on a business trip to
the Soviet Union or attending business conferences with
Russians in other countries. Although English is a
prominent foreign language in Russia and efficient
interpreters are available, these phrases will add another
dimension to your contacts with your Russian-speaking
business associates. The fact that you have made the
effort to master some business expressions will be a
compliment to your hosts.

Good morning. Is the director in?
Доброе утро.
Директор здесь?
DOB-ro-ye OOT-ra.
dee-REHK-tahr zd'yehs'?

**I have an appointment
    with him.**
У меня встреча с ним.
*oo m'ye-N'YA FSTREH-
    cha s' neem.*

Here is my card.
Вот моя визитка.
*VOHT ma-YA vee-ZEET-
    ka.*

125

Thank you.
Спасибо.
spa-SEE-ba.

He is expecting you.
Он ждёт вас.
ohn zhd'yoht vahs.

Welcome to Russia, Mr. Peters.
Добро пожаловать в Советский Союз,
мистер Петерс.
dahb-ROH pa-ZHA-la-vat' f sa-V'YEHT-skee sa-YOOS,
MEES-tehr PEH-tehrs.

How do you like St. Petersburg?
Как вам нравится Петербург?
kahk vahm NRA-vee-tsa pee-t'yehr-BOORG?

Very much.
Очень.
OH-ch'yen'.

It's a marvelous city.
Это замечательный
город.
EH-ta
   za-meh-CHA-tehl'-nee
   GO-rahdt

**We understand
that you want to export
American products into Russia.**
Мы понимаем,
что вы хотите экспортировать
американские товары в Россию.
mee pa-nee-MA-yehm,
shtoh vwee ha-TEE-t'yeh ehx-pahr-TEE-ra-vaht'
ah-meh-ree-KAN-skee-yeh ta-VA-ree v' rahs-SEE-yoo.

Yes. Here is our catalogue showing our latest models
Да. Вот наш каталог
с последними моделями
dah. voht nahsh ka-ta-LOHK
s' pahs-L'YEHD-nee-mee ma-DEH-lya-mee

of computers, videos,
fax machines,
and tape recorders.
компьютеров, видео,
факсов
и магнитофонов.
kam-P'YOO-te-rov,
VEE-deh-oh, FAHK-saf,
ee mahg-nee-ta-FO-nahf.

This other brochure shows
household
and kitchen appliances
Вот другая брошюра
с домашними
и кухонными приспособлениями
voht droo-GAH-ya bra-SH'YU-ra
s' da-MAHSH-nee-mee
ee KOO-kho-nee-mee pree-spa-sahb-L'YEH-nee-ya-mee

and a selection of canned foods.
и набор консервов.
ee na-BOHR kahn-S'YEHR-vahf.

Very attractive.
In our nation
there is much interest
in American products.
Очень привлекательно.
В нашей стране
большой интерес
к американским товарам.
OH-ch'yehn pree-vl'yeh-KA-t'yel'-no.
v' NA-shey stra-N'YEH
bahl'-SHOY een-t'yeh-R'YES
k ah-meh-ree-KAHN-skeem ta-VAH-ram.

Does your company also manufacture
clothing?
Производит ваша компания
одежду?
pra-eez-VOH-deet VA-sha kahm-PA-nee-ya
ah-D'YEHZH-doo?

Certainly.
Here are samples
of sports clothes, "jeans"
Конечно. Вот несколько моделей
спортивной одежды, «джинсы».
ka-N'YESH-shna.
voht N'YEH-skahl'-ka ma-DEH-l'yey
spar-TEEV-nay ah-D'YEHZH-dee, JEAN-see

and also several lines
of cosmetics.
а также несколько наборов
косметики.
ah TAHK-zheh N'YEH-skahl'-ka na-BOH-rahf
kahs-M'YEH-tee-kee.

Thank you.
Спасибо.
spa-SEE-ba.

I will discuss
the purchase of these items
Я буду обсуждать
покупку этих товаров
ya BOO-doo ahp-soo-ZHDAHT'
pa-KOOP-koo EH-teekh ta-VA-rahf

with the government authorities.
с государственными организациями.
z' ga-soo-DAHR-stven-nee-mee ar-ga-nee-ZA-
 tsee-ya-mee.

We are in agreement, aren't we?
Мы договорились, не так ли?
mee da-ga-va-REE-lees', n'yeh tahk lee?

Of course! But we must receive
official permission
before we can make the order.
Конечно! Но мы должны получить
одобрение свыше,
прежде чем делать заказ.
ka-N'YEHSH-na! no mwee dahl-ZHNEE pa-loo-CHEET'
ah-dahb-R'YEH-nee-ye SVEE-sheh,
PREZH-d'yeh ch'yehm D'YEH-laht' za-KAHZ.

We expect a discount of 10%.
What are your terms of payment?
Мы ожидаем скидку на 10%.
Какие условия оплаты?
mwee ah-zhee-DAH-yehm SKEET-koo nah D'YEH-
 s'yaht' prah-TSEN-tahf.
ka-KEE-yeh oos-LO-vee-yah ahp-LA-tee?

By thirty-day bank draft, letter of credit.
Чек должен быть оплачен в тридцать дней,
аккредитив.
check DOHL-zhehn bweet' ahp-LA-ch'yehn f'TREE-
   tsaht' DN'yeh, ak-reh-dee-TEEF.

Is there interest in America
in Russian products?
Есть спрос в Америке
на русские товары?
yest' sprohs v'ah-MEH-ree-k'yeh
na ROOS--skee-yeh ta-VA-ree?

Oh, yes. We are interested
in raw materials:
О, да. Мы заинтересованы
в мырье:
oh, dah. mwee za-een-t'ye-rie-SOH-vah-nee
v see-R'YEH:

lumber, metals, cotton, silk...
древесина, металлы,
хлопок, шёлк...
dr'yeh-v'yeh-SEE-na, meh-TA-lee,
HLO-pok, shohlk...

and manufactured goods
и в промышленных товарых
ee f pra-MWEESH-l'yeh-neeh ta-VA-rahk:

rugs, textiles, furs, vodka, and caviar.
ковры, текстиль, меха, водка и икра.
kahv-REE, tex-TEEL, m'yeh-KHA, VOD-ka ee eek-RA.

We can discuss this tomorrow. Meantime, we would
  like to invite you to dinner today.
Мы обсудим это завтра. Мы хотим пригласить вас
  на ужин сегодня.
*mwee ahp-SOO-deem EH-ta ZAHF-tra. Mwee kha-
  TEEM pree-gla-SEET' vahs na oo-ZHEEN s'yeh-
  VOHD-n'ya.*

Can we call for you at eight?
Можно заехать за вами в восемь?
MO-zhna za-YEH-khaht' za VA-mee v' VO-s'yehm'?

After Dinner

Many thanks for your courtesy.
Большое спасибо за вашу доброту.
bahl'-SHOH-ye spa-SEE-ba za VA-shoo dahb-ra-TOO.

It was a great pleasure to meet you.
Очень приятно познакомиться с вами.
*OH-ch'yehn' pree-YAHT-na paz-na-KO-meet-s'ya s'
  VAH-mee.*

I look forward to doing business with you.
Очень рад сотрудничать с вами.
OH-ch'yehn' RAHT sa-TROOD-nee-chaht s' VAH-mee.

**If you come to America,
let me know in advance.**
Если вы поедете в Америку,
дайте мне знать заранее.
*YEHS-lee vwee pa-YEH-dee-t'yeh v'
   ah-M'YEH-ree-koo,
DAHY-t'yeh m'nyeh znaht' za-RA-nee-yeh.*

**It will be a pleasure
to see you again.**
Будет приятно
увидеть вас снова.
*BOO-d'yeht pree-YAHT-na
oo-VEE-d'yeht' vahs SNO-va.*

**I agree.
Americans and Russians
should be friends.**
Я согласен.
Американцы и русские
должны быть друзьями.
*ya sag-LA-s'yehn. ah-M'YEH-ree-KAHN-tsee ee
   ROOS-kee-yeh
dahl-ZHNEE beet' droozih'-YA-mee.*

**Yes. Long live friendship
between our countries!**
Да. Да здравствует дружба
между нашими странами!
*da. da-ZDRA-stvoo-yeht DROO-zhba
M'YEH-zhdoo NA-shee-me STRA-na-mee!*

23. A New Type of Dictionary

This dictionary supplies a list of English words with their translation into Russian. Only one Russian equivalent is given for each English word—the one most useful to you—so you won't be in doubt regarding which word to use. The phonetic pronunciation is also given for each word so that you will have no difficulty in being understood.

We have detailed some suggestions and shortcuts that will enable you to use this dictionary to form hundreds of correct and useful sentences by yourself.

Each Russian noun is either masculine, feminine, or neuter, and this affects the form of any adjective that precedes it. There is no word for "the" or "a" in Russian, so one uses the noun without the equivalent article. In the dictionary the letters m, f or n in parentheses following the Russian translation of the noun will show you what the gender is.

The nouns listed in the dictionary are given in the nominative case and in the singular. The endings of nouns vary according to how they are used in a sentence.

This is called "case." There are six cases in Russian: nominative (subject), genitive (possessive), dative (indirect object), accusative (direct object), instrumental (the means by which something is done), and locative (prepositional).

Take "Moscow," for example, and its English explanation of the six cases according to the word used in a sentence:

Moscow is beautiful.	(nominative)
Moscow's churches.	(genitive)
An award to Moscow.	(indirect object)
Napoleon burned Moscow.	(direct object)
I was charmed by Moscow.	(instrumental)
In Moscow	(locative)

(Here Moscow is shown only in the singular, because there is only one Moscow). The following table shows the different endings for the three genders of nouns: masculine, feminine, and neuter, both in the singular and the plural.

Here are examples of nouns in their six cases, **singular and plural.**

Noun Cases

Nouns change their endings in the three genders according to their cases, in other words, their use in the sentence.

Masculine
стол (table)

	singular	plural
Nominative	стол	столы
Possessive	стола	столов
Indirect object	столу	столам
Direct object	стол	столы
Instrumental	столом	столами
Locative	столе	столах

Feminine
книга (book)

	singular	plural
Nominative	книга	книги
Possessive	книги	книг
Indirect object	книге	книгам
Direct object	книгу	книги
Instrumental	книгой	книгами
Locative	книге	книгах

Neuter
окно (window)

	singular	plural
Nominative	окно	окна
Possessive	окна	окон
Indirect object	окну	окнам
Direct object	окно	окна
Instrumental	окном	окнами
Locative	окне	окнах

Adjective Cases

Like the noun, the adjective has different endings for each case, but usually they are not the same as the noun endings. Adjectives also change their gender and case according to the noun they modify. You may be relieved to note, however, that adjectives, when used with a word in the plural, take the same adjective endings for all three genders.

большой (big)

Masculine

	singular	plural
Nominative	большой	большие
Possessive	большого	больших
Indirect object	большому	большим
Direct object	большой	большие
Instrumental	большим	большими
Locative	большом	больших

Feminine

	singular	plural
Nominative	большая	большие
Possessive	большой	больших
Indirect object	большой	большим
Direct object	большую	большие
Instrumental	большой	большими
Locative	большой	больших

Neuter

	singular	plural
Nominative	большое	большие
Possessive	большого	больших
Indirect object	большому	большим
Direct object	большое	большие
Instrumental	большим	большими
Locative	большом	больших

Fortunately for the traveler, verbs are relatively easy. The infinitive ends in ть (t') and sometimes ся (s'ya). Here are the endings for говорить (ga-va-REET') "to speak" in the present tense:

I speak	Я говорю	*ya ga-var-YOO*
You speak	Вы говорите	*vwee ga-va-REE-t'yeh*
He (she) speaks	он (она) говорит	*ah (ah-NA) ga-va-REET*
We speak	Мы говорим	*mwee ga-va-REEM*
They speak	Они говорят	*ah-NEE ga-va-R'YAHT*

The past tense of verbs is even simpler, with only four endings to remember: a final -л (l) for "I" (m), and "he," -ла (la) for "she," -ло (lo) and ли (*EE-lee*) for "you," "we," and "they."

An easy way to ask questions is to use ли (lee):

Do you speak Russian?   (*ga-va-REE-t'yeh lee vwee pa-ROOS-kee?*)

The imperative form is the basic stem plus те (*t'yeh*). This is the "polite" imperative, the best one for a foreign visitor to use, as in "Tell me"—скажите мне—(*ska-ZHEET-yeh mn'yeh*). And here is some good news: There is no present form of "to be" although the past and future forms do exist. The past of "to be" is:

I was (m), I was (f)	я был, я была	(*ya beel*) (*ya-bee-LA*)
He was, she was, it was	он был, она была, это было	(*ohn beel*) (*ah-NA bee-LA*) (*ah-no BEE-lo*)
You were	вы были	(*vwee BEE-lee*)
We were	мы были	(*mwee BEE-lee*)
They were	они были	(*ah-NEE BEE-lee*)

For some verbs the future tense is formed quite simply by using combined with the infinitive of the verb "will." This is the "imperfective" aspect of the verb.

I will write	Я буду писать	*ya BOO-doo pee-SAHT'*
He (she) will write	Он/она будет писать	*ohn/ah-NA BOO-d'yet pee-SAHT'*
You will write	Вы будете писать	*vwee BOO-d'yeh-t'yeh pee-SAHT'*
We will write	Мы будем писать	*mwee BOO-d'yem pee-SAHT'*
They will write	Они будеут писать	*ah-NEE BOO-doot pee-SAHT'*

The two "aspects" of the Russian verb are called the "perfective" and the "imperfective"; perfective verbs are used only in the past or future. The perfective verb in the past consists of the past tense of the verb preceded by a corresponding special preposition. For the future, this same preposition is combined with the present form of the verb. The use of these prepositional prefixes changes the meaning of the verb as to whether the action was or will be going on (imperfective) or whether it was definitely completed or will be completed (perfective).

Some of the prepositions that characterize the perfective verbs are под (*pohd*), при (*pree*), с (*s*), от (*oht*), на (*na*), по (*poh*), за (*za*).

The appropriate preposition is written together with the verb as one word and the first syllable and serves as a signal to recognize the perfective when you see or hear them.

To illustrate the difference between the perfective and the imperfective: If you are reading a book, you use the verb читать; if you have read it through, the verb becomes прочитать. Thus the first example is imperfective and the latter, perfective. Consider a historical example of action: "He shot the Tsar" **Он стрелял в царя** does not show whether or not the shot was final or fatal (imperfective), but if **застрелил** were used, it would indicate that the Tsar died from the shot at the time.

These aspects of the verb and the cases and agreement of nouns and adjectives are points of the Russian language that will become natural to you through practice, just as they do to native Russians. Actually, although they may seem difficult, they are logical and time saving, considering the additional subordinate phrases neccessary to express the same concept in English and a number of Western languages. Russian has a certain advantage of linguistic precision and of providing a more exact meaning of the verb to time, probability, and state of action.

Perhaps this linguistic way of thinking has proved a helpful legacy to Russians in scientific development both here—and in space.

Dictionary

A _____

about	о, об	*oh, ohb*
above	над	*naht*
abroad	за границей	*za gra-NEE-tsay*
(to be) absent	отсутствовать	*aht-SOOT-stvah-vaht'*
absolutely	совершенно	*sa-vehr-SHEHN-na*
academy	академия (f)	*ah-ka-D'YEH-mee-ya*
accent	акцент (m)	*ahk-TSENT*
(to) accept	принять	*pree-N'YAHT'*
accident (vehicle)	авария (f)	*ah-VA-ree-ya*
account	счёт (m)	*s'choht*
(to) ache	болеть	*ba-L'YEHT'*
across	через	*CH'EH-rehs*
actor	актёр (m)	*ahk-T'YOHR*
actress	актриса (f)	*ahk-TREE-sa*
address	адрес (m)	*AH-dres*
(to) admire	восхищаться	*vahs-heesh-CHAHT-sa*
admission	допуск (m)	*DOH-poosk*
adult	взрослый	*vz-ROHS-lee*
advertisement	объявление (n)	*ahb-yahv-L'EH-nee-yeh*
advice	совет (m)	*sa-V'YET*
(to be) afraid	бояться	*ba-YAHT-sa*
Africa	Африка	*AH-free-ka*
after	после	*POHS-l'yeh*
afternoon	полдень (m)	*POHL-d'yen'*
agent	агент	*ah-GHENT*
ago	тому назад	*ta-MOO na-ZAHT*
(to) agree	соглашаться	*sa-gla-SHAHT-sa*
I agree	Я согласен (m)	*ya sa-GLA-s'yehn*
	Я согласна (f)	*ya sa-GLA-snah*
air	воздух (m)	*VOHZ-dookh*
airplane	самолёт (m)	*sah-mah-L'YOHT*
airport	аэропорт (m)	*a-eh-rah-POHRT*

all	всё, все	*fs'yoh, fs'yeh*
allow	разрешать	*rahz-reh-SHAHT'*
all right	хорошо	*khah-rah-SHOH*
already	уже	*oo-ZHEH*
also	тоже	*TOH-zheh*
although	хотя	*khah-t'YAH*
always	всегда	*f'sehg-DA*
America	Америка	*ah-MEH-ree-kah*
American (m, f)	американец (m)	*ah-meh-ree-KAH-netz*
	американка (f)	*ah-meh-ree-KAHN-kah*
amount	сумма (f)	*SOOM-ma*
amusing	забавный	*zah-BAHV-nee*
and	и	*ee*
(to be) angry	сердиться	*s'yehr-DEET-sa*
animal	животное (n)	*zhee-VOHT-noh-yeh*
annoying	раздражительный	*rahz-drah-ZHEEH-tehl'-nee*
answer	ответ (m)	*aht-V'YEHT*
antiseptic	антисептик (m)	*ahn-tee-SEP-teek*
anything	что-либо	*SH'TOH-lee-ba*
apartment	квартира (f)	*k'vahr-TEE-ra*
apple	яблоко (n)	*YAH-blah-ka*
appointment	встреча (f)	*fs't-REH-cha*
April	апрель (m)	*ah-PREHL'*
Arab	араб (m)	*ah-RAHP*
architect	архитектор (m)	*ahr-hee-TECK-tor*
architecture	архитектура (f)	*ahr-hee-teck-TOO-ra*
arm	рука (f)	*roo-KAH*
army	армия (f)	*AHR-mee-ya*
(to) arrange	устроить	*oos-TRO-eet'*
(to) arrest	арестовать	*ah-reh-stah-VAHT'*
(to) arrive	прибывать	*pree-bee-VAHT'*
art	искусство	*ees-KOOST-va*
artist	художник (m)	*khoo-DOHZH-nick*
	художница (f)	*khoo-DOHZH-nit-sa*
as	так как, как	*TAHK kahk, kahk*
Asia	Азия	*AH-z'ya*

(to) ask	спрашивать	*SPRAH-shee-vaht'*
(to) ask for	просить	*prah-SEET'*
aspirin	аспирин (m)	*ahs-pee-REEN*
at	в	*v*
Atlantic Ocean	Атлантический океан	*aht-lahn-TEE-chess-kee ah-keh-AHN*
Attention!	Внимание!	*vnee-MA-nee-yeh!*
August	август (m)	*AHV-goost*
aunt	тётя (f)	*T'YO-t'ya*
Australia	Австралия	*ahf-STRA-lee-ya*
Australian (m, f)	Австралиец (m)	*ahf-stra-LEE-yets*
	Австралийка (f)	*ahf-stra-LEE-ka*
Austria	Австрия	*AHF-stree-ya*
Austrian (m, f)	Австриец (m)	*ahf-STREE-yets*
	Австрийка (f)	*ahf-STREE-ka*
author	автор (m)	*AHF-tohr*
automatic	автоматический	*ahf-tah-mah-TEE-cheh-skee*
autumn	осень (f)	*oh-S'YEHN'*

B _____

bachelor	холостяк (m)	*khah-lah-ST'YAHK*
back (adv.)	назад	*nah-ZAHT*
I will be back	Я вернусь.	*ya v'yehr-NOOS'*
back (n.)	спина (f)	*spee-NA*
bad (adj.)	плохой	*plah-HOY*
badly (adv.)	плохо	*PLOH-ha*
baggage	багаж (m)	*bah-GAHZH*
bandage	бинт (m)	*beent*
bank	банк (m)	*bahnk*
bar	бар (m)	*bahr*
bath	ванна (f)	*VAHN-na*
bathing suit	купальный костюм (m)	*koo-PAHL'-nee ka-STYOOM*

bathroom	ванная (f)	*VAHN-na-ya*
battery	батарея (f)	*ba-ta-R'YEH-ya*
battle	сражение (n)	*sra-ZHEN-nee-yeh*
(to) be	быть	*beet'*
beach	пляж (m)	*pl'YAHZH*
beard	борода (f)	*ba-rah-DAH*
beautiful	красивый	*kra-SEE-vee*
because	потому что	*pa-ta-MOO shtoh*
bed	постель (f)	*pa-st'YEHL'*
bedroom	спальня (f)	*SPAHL'-n'ya*
beef	говядина (f)	*ga-V'YA-dee-na*
beer	пиво (n)	*PEE-vah*
before (place, time)	перед, до	*P'YEH-r'yet, doh*
(to) begin	начинать	*na-chee-NAHT'*
behind	за, сзади	*za, ZZA-dee*
Belgian	Бельгиец (m)	*behl'-GHEE-yets*
	Бельгийка (f)	*behl'-GHEE-ka*
Belgium	Бельгия	*BEHL'-ghee-ya*
(to) believe	верить	*V'YEH-reet'*
below (prep.)	под	*poht*
beside	около	*OH-ka-la*
best	лучший	*LOOCH-chee*
better	лучшее	*LOOCH-sheh*
between	между	*M'YEHZH-doo*
big	большой	*bol'-SHOY*
bill	счёт (m)	*SH'CHOHT*
bird	птица (f)	*PTEE-tsah*
birthday	день рождения	*d'yen' rahzh-'DYEH-nee-ya*
black	чёрный	*CH'YOHR-nee*
blanket	одеяло (n)	*ah-d'yeh-YA-lah*
blood	кровь (f)	*krohf'*
blouse	блуза (f)	*BLOO-za*
boat	лодка (f)	*LOH-tka*
bomb	бомба (f)	*BOHM-ba*
book	книга (f)	*KNEE-ga*

bookstore	книжный магазин	*KNEEZH-nee ma-ga-ZEEN*
boss	босс (m)	*BOHSS*
both	оба (m), обе (f)	*OH-ba, OH-b'yeh*
bottle	бутылка (f)	*boo-TEEL-ka*
bottom	дно (n)	*d'no*
boy	мальчик (m)	*MAHL'-chik*
brains	мозги (pl.)	*mahz-GHEE*
brake	тормоз (m)	*TOHR-mahs*
brave	храбрый	*KHRA-bree*
bread	хлеб (m)	*KHL'yep*
(to) break	ломать	*la-MAHT'*
breakfast	завтрак (m)	*ZAHF-trahk*
to breathe	дышать	*dee-SHAHT'*
bridge	мост (m)	*mohst*
bridge (card game)	бридж (m)	*bredzh*
briefcase	портфель (m)	*port-FEHL'*
(to) bring	приносить	*pree-nah-SEET'*
Bring me (something)	принесите мне...	*pree-neh-SEET-yeh mn'YEH*
broken	сломанный	*SLOH-ma-nee*
brother	брат (m)	*braht*
brown	коричневый	*ka-REECH-n'yeh-vee*
brush	щётка (f)	*SH'CHOHT-ka*
building	здание (n)	*ZDAH-n'yeh*
bus	автобус (m)	*ahf-TOH-boos*
bus stop	автобусная остановка	*ahf-TOH-boo-sna-ya ah-sta-NOHV-ka*
business	бизнес	*BEE-znehs*
(I am) busy (m)	я занят	*ya ZA-n'yaht*
but	но	*no*
butter	масло (n)	*MAHS-lo*
button	пуговица (f)	*POO-ga-vee-tsa*
(to) buy	покупать	*pa-koo-PAHT'*
by	возле	*VOHZ-l'yeh*

C

cabbage	капуста (f)	*ka-POO-sta*
cake	торт (m)	*tort*
(to) call (telephone)	звонить	*zva-NEET'*
Call me!	Позвоните мне! (polite)	*pa-zvah-NEE-t'yeh mn'yeh!*
camera	фотоаппарат (m)	*fo-toh-ah-pa-RAHT*
can (to be able to)	мочь	*mohch*
can you...?	Можете ли вы?..	*MO-zheh-t'yeh lee vwee..?*
I can	Я могу	*ya ma-GOO*
I can't	Я не могу	*yah n'yeh ma-GOO*
can opener	открывалка (f)	*aht-kree-VAHL-ka*
Canada	Канада	*ka-NA-da*
Canadian	Канадец (m)	*ka-NA-d'yehts*
	Канадка (f)	*ka-NAHD-ka*
capitalism	капитализм (m)	*ka-pee-ta-LEEZM*
captain	капитан (m)	*ka-pee-TAHN*
car	машина (f)	*ma-SHEE-na*
carburetor	карбюратор (m)	*kar-byo-RA-tor*
cards	карты	*KAR-tee*
careful (adj.)	осторожный	*ah-sta-ROHZH-nee*
Be careful!	Будьте осторожны!	*BOOD'-t'ye ahs-ta-ROHZH-nee!*
carrot	морковь (f)	*mar-KOHF'*
(to) carry	нести	*ness-TEE*
cashier	кассир (m)	*ka-SEER*
cathedral	собор (m)	*sa-BOHR*
Catholic	католический	*ka-ta-LEE-cheh-skee*
ceiling	потолок (m)	*pa-ta-LOHK*
cemetery	кладбище (n)	*KLAHD-beesh-cheh*
centimeter	сантиметр (m)	*sahn-tee-MEHTR*

century	век (m)	*v'yek*
certainly	конечно	*ka-N'YEH-chna*
chair	стул (m)	*stool*
(to) change (money)	разменять	*rahz-me-N'YAHT'*
(to) change	изменить	*eez-mee-NEET'*
cheap	дешевый	*de-SHO-vee*
check (money)	чек (m)	*check*
(to) check in (hotel)	зарегистрироваться	*za-re-ghee-STREE-ra-vaht'-s'ya*
cheese	сыр (m)	*SEER*
child	ребёнок (m)	*re-B'YO-nahk*
China	Китай	*kee-TAI*
Chinese	Китаец (m)	*kee-TA-yets*
	Китаянка (f)	*kee-ta-YAHN-ka*
chocolate	шоколад (m)	*sha-ka-LAHT*
Christian	христианин (m)	*khrees-T'YA-neen*
	христианка (f)	*khrees-T'YA-neen-ka*
church	церковь (f)	*TSEHR-kaf*
cigarette	сигарета (f)	*see-ga-RE-ta*
C.I.S. (Commonwealth of Independent States)	СНГ	*ES-EN-GAY*
citizen	гражданин (m)	*grahzh-da-NEEN*
	гражданка (f)	*grahzh-DAHN-ka*
city	город (m)	*GO-raht*
clean	чистый	*CHEES-tee*
(to) clean	чистить	*CHEES-teet'*
clever	умный	*OOM-nee*
clock	часы (pl.)	*cha-SEE*
close	близко	*BLEES-ka*
(to) close	закрыть	*za-KREET'*
closed	закрыто	*za-KREE-ta*

clothes	одежда (sing.) (f)	ah-D'YEHZH-da
coast	берег (m)	B'YE-r'yek
coat (overcoat)	пальто (n)	pahl'TOH
coffee	кофе (m)	KO-feh
cold (sickness)	простуда (f)	prahs-TOO-da
cold	холодный	kha-LOHD-nee
colonel	полковник (m)	pahl-KOHV-neek
color	цвет	tsv'yet
company	компания (f)	kahm-PA-nee-ya
communist	коммунист (m)	ka-moo-NEEST
	коммунистка (f)	ka-moo-NEEST-ka
competition	соревнование (n)	sa-rehv-na-VA-n'yeh
computer	компьютер (m)	kahm-P'YOO-tehr
concert	концерт (m)	kahn-TSEHRT
congratulations!	Поздравляю!	pahz-drahv-L'YA-yoo!
consul	консул (m)	KOHN-sool
continent	континент (m)	kahn-tee-NEHNT
contract	контракт (m)	kahn-TRAHKT
conversation	беседа (f)	bee-SEH-da
(to) cook	готовить	ga-TO-veet'
copy	копия (f)	KO-pee-yah
corner	угол (m)	OO-gahl
correct	правильный	PRA-veel'-nee
(to) cost	стоить	STOH-eet'
cotton	хлопок (m)	KHLO-pahk
cough	кашель (m)	KA-shehl'
country	страна (f)	stra-NA
cow	корова (f)	ka-RO-va
crazy	сумасшедший	soo-ma-SHET-shee
(to) cry	плакать	PLA-kaht'
(to) cross	пересекать	peh-reh-seh-KAHT'
cup	чашка (f)	CHAHSH-ka
customs (pl.)	таможня (f) (sing.)	ta-MOHZH-n'ya
(to) cut	резать	R'YEH-zaht'

D

(to) dance	танцевать	*tahn-tseh-VAHT'*
dangerous	опасно	*ah-PA-sna*
dark	темно	*t'yehm-NO*
date (calendar)	число (n)	*chees-LO*
date (meeting)	свидание (n)	*svee-DA-nee-yeh*
daughter	дочь (f)	*dohch'*
day	день (m)	*d'yen'*
dead	мёртвый	*M'YORT-vwee*
dear	дорогой	*da-ra-GOY*
(my) dear	(мой) дорогой (m)	*(moy) da-ra-GOY*
	(моя) дорогая (f)	*(ma-YA) da-ra-GA-ya*
December	декабрь (m)	*d'yeh-KABR'*
(to) decide	решить	*reh-SHEE-t'*
deep	глубокий	*gloo-BO-kee*
deer	олень (m)	*ah-L'YEN'*
delay	задержка (f)	*za-D'YEHRZH-ka*
delicious	вкусный	*VKOOS-nee*
delighted	рад (m) рада (f)	*raht (m) RA-da (f)*
delivery	доставка (f)	*da-STAHF-ka*
democracy	демократия (f)	*de-mo-KRA-tee-ya*
dentist	дантист (m)	*dahn-TEEST*
departure	отъезд (m)	*aht-YEZD*
(to) describe	описать	*ah-pee-SAHT'*
dessert	сладкое (n)	*SLAHT-ko-yeh*
(to) develop	развивать	*rahz-vee-VAHT'*
devil	чёрт (m)	*ch'yort*
dictionary	словарь (m)	*sla-VAR'*
different (one)	другой (m)	*droo-GOY*
	другая (f)	*droo-GA-ya*
difficult	трудный	*TROOD-nee*
to dine	обедать	*ah-BEH-daht'*
dining room	столовая (f)	*sta-LO-va-ya*
dinner	ужин (m)	*OO-zheen*

direction	направление (n)	na-prahv-L'YEH-nee-yeh
director/ manager	директор (m)	dee-REHK-tor
dirty	грязный	GR'YAHZ-nee
disappointed	разочарованный	ra-zo-cha-RO-va-nee
discount	скидка (f)	SKEET-ka
distance	расстояние (n)	rahs-sta-YA-nee-yeh
(to be) divorced	развестись	rahz-vehs-TEES'
to do	делать	D'YEH-laht'
Do you understand?	Вы понимаете?	vwee pa-nee-MA-yeh-teh?
doctor	врач (m)	vrahch
dog	собака (f)	sa-BA-ka
dollar	доллар (m)	DOHL-lar
donkey	осёл (m)	ah-S'YOHL
Don't do that!	Не делайте это!	n'yeh D'YEH-la-ee-t'yeh EH-ta!
Don't go!	Не ходите!	n'yeh ha-DEE-t'yeh!
I don't have...	У меня нет...	oo meh-YA n'yeht...
door	дверь (f)	dv'yehr'
down (direction)	вниз	vneez
dress (n)	платье (f)	PLA-t'yeh
(to) drink	пить	peet'
(to) drive (a car)	водить	va-DEET'
driver	водитель (m)	va-DEE-tehl'
driver's license	водительские права	va-DEE-tehl'-skee'yeh pra-VA
drunk	пьяный	p'YA-nee
Dutch (m,f)	голландец (m)	ga-LAHN-d'yehts
	голландка (f)	ga-LAHNT-ka

E _____

each	каждый	KAHZH-dee
ear	ухо (n)	OO-ha

early	рано	*RA-na*
(to) earn	зарабатывать	*za-ra-BA-tee-vaht'*
earth	земля (f)	*zehm-L'YA*
east	восток (m)	*va-STOCK*
(to) eat	есть	*yest'*
egg (sing.)	яйцо (n)	*yai-TSO*
eggs (pl.)	яйца (pl.)	*YAI-tsa*
eight	восемь	*VO-s'yem'*
eighteen	восемнадцать	*va-s'yem-NAT-sat'*
eighty	восемьдесят	*VO-s'yehm-deh-s'yaht'*
electric	электрический	*eh-lek-TREE-chess-kee*
elephant	слон (m)	*slohn*
elevator	лифт (m)	*lift*
eleven	одиннадцать	*ah-DEE-naht-tsaht'*
else (more)	ещё	*yesh-CHO*
embassy	посольство (n)	*pa-SOHL'-st'va*
embroidery	вышивка (f)	*VEE-sheef-ka*
emergency	экстренный случай	*EHK-strehn-nee SLOO-chai*
employee	наёмный рабочий	*na-YOHM-nee ra-BO-chee*
employer	работодатель (m)	*ra-bo-ta-DA-t'yehl'*
end	конец (m)	*ka-N'YETS*
(to) end	заканчивать	*za-KAHN-chee-vaht'*
England	Англия	*AHN-glee-ya*
English (adj.)	английский	*ahn-GLEES-kee*
English (m, f)	англичанин (m)	*ahn-glee-CHAHN-neen*
	англичанка (f)	*ahn-glee-CHAHN-ka*
entertaining	развлекательный	*rahz-v'leh-KA-tehl-nee*
enough	достаточно	*dahs-TA-toch-na*
error	ошибка (f)	*ah-SHEEP-ka*
especially	особенно	*ah-SO-behn-na*
Europe	Европа	*yehv-RO-pa*
European	европеец (m)	*yehv-ro-P'YEH-yets*
	европейка (f)	*yehv-ro-P'YEH-ka*
evening	вечер (m)	*V'YEH-cher*
every	каждый	*KAHZH-dee*

everybody (sing.)	все (pl.)	*fs'yeh*
everything (sing.)	всё (sing.)	*fs'yo*
exactly	точно	*TOHCH-na*
excellent	отлично	*aht-LEECH-na*
except	кроме	*KRO-m'yeh*
(to) exchange	менять	*m'yeh-N'YAHT'*
Excuse me!	Извините!	*eez-vee-NEE-t'yeh!*
exercise	упражнение (n)	*oo-prahzh-N'YEH-nee-yeh*
exit	выход (m)	*vwee-hot*
expensive	дорогой	*da-ra-GOY*
experience	опыт (m)	*OH-pweet*
explanation	объяснение (n)	*ahb-yahs-N'YEH-nee-yeh*
(to) export	экспортировать	*ex-par-TEE-ra-vaht'*
express train	скорый поезд	*SKO-ree PO-yezt*
extra	дополнительный	*da-pahl-NEE-tehl'-nee*
eye	глаз (m)	*glahs*
eyes	глаза (pl.)	*gla-ZA*

F _____

face	лицо (n)	*lee-TSO*
factory	завод (m)	*za-VOHT*
(to) fall	падать	*PA-daht'*
family	семья (f)	*s'yeh-M'YA*
famous	известный	*eez-V'YEHST-nee*
far	далеко	*da-l'yeh-KO*
How far?	Как далеко?	*kahk da-lee-KO?*
farm	ферма (f)	*FEHR-ma*
farther	дальше	*DAHL'-sheh*
fast	быстро	*BWEE-strah*
father	отец (m)	*ah-T'YETS*
February	февраль (m)	*f'yeh-VRAHL'*
(to) feel	чувствовать	*CHOOST-va-vaht'*

female	женский	ZHEN-skee
fever	жар (m)	zhar
few	мало	MA-la
field	поле (n)	PO-l'yeh
fifteen	пятнадцать	p'yah-NAHT-saht'
fifty	пятьдесят	p'yaht-d'yeh-S'YAHT
(to) fight	драться	DRAHT-s'ya
(to) fill	наполнять	na-pahl-N'YAHT'
film (photo)	плёнка (f)	PL'YOHN-ka
film (movie)	фильм (m)	film
finally	окончательно	ah-kahn-CHA-t'yehl'-na
(to) find)	находить	na-ha-DEET)
(to) find out	узнать	oo-ZNAHT'
finger	палец (m)	PA-l'yets
(to) finish	кончать	kahn-CHAHT'
Finland	Финляндия	feen-L'YAHN-dee-ya
fire	огонь (m)	ah-GOHN'
first	первый	P'YEHR-vee
(to) fish	ловить рыбу	la-VEET' REE-boo
(to) fit	подходить	paht-ha-DEET'
five	пять	p'YAHT'
flag	флаг (m)	flahk
flight	полёт (m)	pa-L'YOHT
floor	пол (m)	pohl
flower	цветок (m)	ts'v'yeh-TOHK
(to) fly	летать	leh-TAHT'
fly	муха (f)	MOO-kha
food	пища (f)	PEESH-cha
foot	ступня (f)	stoop-NYA
for	для	dl'ya
foreigner	иностранец (m)	ee-na-STRA-nyets
	иностранка (f)	ee-na-STRAHN-ka
forest	лес (m)	l'yes
(to) forget	забывать	za-bee-VAHT'
Don't forget!	Не забудьте!	n'yeh za-BOOT-t'yeh!
fork	вилка (f)	VEEL-ka

forty	сорок	*SO-rahk*
fountain	фонтан (m)	*fahn-TAHN*
four	четыре	*ch'yeh-TEE-reh*
fourteen	четырнадцать	*ch'yeh-TEER-naht-tsaht*
fox	лиса (f)	*lee-SA*
France	Франция	*FRAHN-ts'ya*
free	свободный	*sva-BOHD-nee*
freedom	свобода (f)	*sva-BO-da*
French (adj.)	французский	*frahn-TSOOS-kee*
French (m, f)	француз (m)	*frahn-TSOOZ*
	француженка (f)	*frahn-TSOO-zhen-ka*
frequently	часто	*CHA-sta*
fresh	свежий	*SV'YEH-zhee*
Friday	пятница (f)	*P'YAHT-nee-tsa*
fried	жареный	*ZHA-reh-nee*
friend	друг (m)	*drook*
from	от	*oht*
(in) front of	перед	*P'YEH-reht*
frozen	замороженный	*za-ma-RO-zheh-nee*
fruit	фрукты (pl.)	*FROOK-tee*
full	полный	*POL-nee*
funny	смешной	*smesh-NOY*
fur	мех (m)	*m'yekh*
future	будущее (n)	*BOO-doosh-cheh-yeh*

G _____

game	игра (f)	*ee-GRA*
garage	гараж (m)	*ga-RAHZH*
garden	сад (m)	*saht*
garlic	чеснок (m)	*chess-NOK*
gasoline	бензин (m)	*ben-ZEEN*
gas station	бензоколонка (f)	*ben-za-ka-LON-ka*
general	генерал (m)	*geh-neh-RAHL*
generally	вообще	*va-ahp-SH'CHEH*

generous	щедрый	*SH'CHEH-dree*
genuine	настоящий	*nah-sta-YASH-chee*
German (adj.)	немецкий	*n'yeh-METS-kee*
German (m, f)	немец (m)	*N'YEH-mets*
	немка	*N'YEHM-ka*
Germany	Германия (f)	*gehr-MA-nee-ya*
(to) get (obtain)	достать	*dahs-TAHT'*
(to) get off	сходить	*s'ha-DEET'*
(to) get on (into)	садиться	*sa-DEET-s'ya*
(to) get up	вставать	*fsta-VAHT'*
gift	подарок (m)	*pa-DA-rahk*
girl	девушка (f)	*D'YEH-voosh-ka*
(to) give	давать	*da-VAHT'*
Give me . . .	Дайте мне . . .	*DAI-t'yeh mn'yeh . . .*
glad	доволен (m)	*da-VO-l'yehn*
	довольна (f)	*da-VOHL'-na*
(eye) glasses	очки (pl.)	*ahch-KEE*
glove	перчатка (f)	*pehr-CHAHT-ka*
(to) go (on foot)	идти	*eet-TEE*
(to) go (by vehicle)	ехать	*YEH-haht'*
I go	Я иду	*ya ee-DOO*
You go	Вы идёте	*vwee ee-D'YO-t'yeh*
We go	Мы идём	*mwee ee-D'YOHM*
They go	Они идут	*ah-NEE ee-DOOT*
He, she, it goes	Он, она, оно/идёт	*on, ah-NA, ah-NO ee-D'YOHT*
(to) go away	уходить	*oo-ha-DEET'*
Go away!	Уйдите!	*ooee-DEE-t'yeh!*
God	бог (m)	*bohk*
gold	золото (n)	*ZO-la-ta*
good	хорошо	*ha-ra-SHO*
Good-bye!	До свидания!	*da svee-DAHN-ya!*
good-looking	красивый	*kra-SEE-vwee*
government	правительство (n)	*pra-VEE-tehl'-st'va*
grandfather	дедушка (m)	*D'YEH-doosh-ka*

grandmother	бабушка (f)	*BA-boosh-ka*
grapes (pl.)	виноград (sing.)	*vee-na-GRAHT*
grateful	благодарный	*bla-ga-DAR-nee*
gray	серый	*S'YEH-ree*
great	великий	*v'yeh-LEE-kee*
green	зелёный	*zeh-L'YO-nee*
group	группа (f)	*GROUP-pa*
guest	гость (m)	*gost'*
guide	гид (m)	*geet*
gun (rifle)	ружьё (m)	*roo-ZH'YO*

H _____

hair (sing.)	волосы (pl.)	*VO-la-see*
hairbrush	расчёска (f)	*rahs-CH'YO-ska*
hairdresser's	парикмахерская (f)	*pa-reek-MA-khehr-ska-ya*
haircut	стрижка (f)	*STREEZH-ka*
half	половина (f)	*pa-la-VEE-na*
hammer	молоток (m)	*ma-la-TOHK*
hand	рука (f)	*roo-KA*
(to) happen	случаться	*sloo-CHANT-sa*
What is happening?	В чём дело?	*f' ch'yohm D'YEH-la?*
happy	счастливый	*schahs-LEE-vee*
hard (difficult)	трудно	*TROOD-na*
hat	шляпа (f)	*SHL'YA-pa*
(to) have	иметь	*ee-M'YEHT'*
I (we, you, they) have	У меня (нас, вас, них) есть	*oo m'yeh-N'YA (nahs, vahs, neeh) yehst'*
he, (it, she) has	У него (неё) есть	*oo n'yeh-VO (n'yeh-YO) yest'*
Have you...?	У вас есть...?	*oo vahs yest' ...?*
he	он	*ohn*
head	голова (f)	*ga-la-VA*

(to) hear	слышать	*SLEE-shaht'*
heart	сердце (n)	*SEHR-tseh*
heat	жара (f)	*zha-RAH*
heavy	тяжёлый (m)	*t'ya-ZHO-lee*
Hello! (phone)	Алло!	*ahl-LO!*
(to) help	помогать	*pa-ma-GAHT'*
Help!	Помогите!	*pa-ma-GEE-t'yeh!*
her (direct object)	её	*yeh-YO*
to her	ей	*yay*
her (possessive)	её	*yeh-YO*
here	здесь	*zd'yehs'*
high	высокий	*vee-SO-kee*
highway	шоссе (n)	*shohs-SEH*
hill	холм (m)	*hohlm*
him (dir. obj.)	его	*yeh-VO*
to him	ему	*yeh-MOO*
his (poss.)	его	*yeh-VO*
history	история (f)	*ees-TOH-ree-ya*
holiday	праздник (m)	*PRAHZ-nik*
Holland	Голла́ндия	*ga-LAHN-dee-ya*
(at) home	дома	*DOH-ma*
honey	мёд (m)	*m'yoht*
(to) hope	надеяться	*na-D'YEH-yaht-sa*
horse	лошадь (f)	*LO-shaht'*
hospital	больница (f)	*bahl'-NEE-tsa*
hot	жарко	*ZHAR-ka*
hotel	гостиница (f)	*gahs-TEE-nee-tsa*
hour	час (m)	*chahs*
house	дом (m)	*dohm*
how	как	*kahk*
How far?	Как далеко?	*kahk dah-lee-KO?*
How much?	Сколько?	*SKOHL'-ka?*
however	однако	*ahd-NA-ka*
hundred	сто	*stoh*

Hungary	Венгрия (f)	*VEHN-gree-ya*
Hungarian	венгр (m)	*vehngr*
(m, f)	венгерка (f)	*vehn-GEHR-ka*
hungry	голодный	*ga-LOHD-nee*
(to) hurry	спешить	*spe-SHEET'*
Hurry up!	Скорее!	*ska-R'YEH-yeh!*
husband	муж (m)	*moozh*

I _____

I	Я	*ya*
ice	лёд (m)	*l'yoht*
ice cream	мороженое (n)	*ma-RO-zheh-no-yeh*
idea	идея (f)	*ee-D'YEH-ya*
identity card	удостоверение	*oo-dahs-ta-veh-R'YEH-*
	личности	*nee-yeh LEECH-nahs-tee*
idiot	идиот (m)	*ee-dee-OHT*
if	если	*YEHS-lee*
(to) import	ввозить	*v'vah-ZEET'*
imported	импортный	*EEMppart-nee*
important	важный	*VAHZH-nee*
impossible (adv.)	невозможно	*n'yeh-vahz-MOHZH-nah*
in	в	*v'*
including	включая	*fkl'yoo-CHA-ya*
incorrect	неправильный	*n'yeh-PRA-veel'-nee*
independent	независимый	*n'yeh-za-VEE-see-mee*
India	Индия	*EEN-dee-ya*
Indian (m, f)	индиец (m)	*een-DEE-yehts*
	индианка (f)	*een-dee-AHN-ka*
industry	промышленность (f)	*pra-MEESH-len-nost'*
information	информация (f)	*een-far-MA-ts'ya*
injury	ранение (n)	*ra-N'YEH-nee-yeh*
inquiry	расследование (n)	*rahs-SLEH-da-va-nee-yeh*
inside	внутри	*v'noo-TREE*

instead	вместо	*VM'YEH-sta*
intelligent	умный	*OOM-nee*
interested	заинтересованный	*za-een-teh-reh-SO-va-nee*
interesting	интересно	*een-teh-R'YEH-sna*
international	международный	*mehzh-doo-na-ROHD-nee*
interpreter	переводчик	*p'yeh-r'yeh-VOHT-chik*
into	в	*v'*
(to) introduce	знакомить	*zna-KO-meet'*
May I	Разрешите мне	*rahz-reh-SHEE-t'yeh*
introduce...	представить...	*mn'yeh*
		preht-STA-veet' ...
invitation	приглашение (n)	*pree-gla-SHE-n'yeh*
(to) iron	гладить	*GLA-deet'*
island	остров (m)	*OHS-trahf*
it (is)	это	*EH-ta*
Italian (adj.)	итальянский	*ee-ta-L'YAHN-skee*
Italian (m, f)	итальянец (m)	*ee-ta-L'YA-n'yets*
	итальянка (f)	*ee-ta-L'YAHN-ka*
Italy	Италия (f)	*ee-TA-lee-ya*

J ———————————————————

jacket	пиджак (m)	*peet-ZHAHK*
January	январь (m)	*yahn-VAHR'*
Japan	Япония (f)	*ya-POHN-ee-ya*
Japanese (m, f)	японец (m)	*ya-PO-n'yets*
	японка (f)	*ya-POHN-ka*
jewelry	драгоценности (f)	*dra-ga-TSEN-na-stee*
Jew (m, f)	еврей (m)	*yehv-RAY*
	Еврейка (f)	*yehv-RAY-ka*
job	работа (f)	*ra-BO-ta*
joke	шутка (f)	*SHOOT-ka*
(to) joke	шутить	*shoo-TEET'*
July	июль (m)	*ee-YOOL'*
June	июнь (m)	*ee-YOON'*

just (only)	только	*TOHL'-ka*
just (just now)	только что	*TOHL'-ka shtoh*
justice	справедливость (f)	*spra-ved-LEE-vahst'*

K _____

(to) keep	хранить	*hra-NEET'*
Keep out!	Не входить!	*n'ye f'h-ADEET'!*
key	ключ (m)	*kl'yooch*
to kill	убивать	*oo-bee-VAHT'*
kilometer	километр (m)	*kee-la-M'YEHTR*
kind	добрый	*DOH-bree*
king	король (m)	*ka-ROHL'*
kiss	поцелуй (m)	*pa-tseh-LOO-ee*
kitchen	кухня (f)	*KOOKH-n'ya*
knee	колено (n)	*ka-LEH-na*
knife	нож (m)	*nohsh*
(to) know	знать	*znaht'*
Do you know...?	Вы знаете...?	*vwee ZNA-ee-t'yeh...?*
Who knows?	Кто знает?	*ktoh ZNA-yeht?*

L _____

ladies' room	женский туалет	*ZHEHN-skee too-ah-L'YEHT*
lake	озеро (n)	*OH-z'yeh-ra*
lamb	барашек (m)	*ba-RA-shek*
land	земля (f)	*z'yehm-L'YA*
(to) land	приземляться	*pree-z'yehm-L'YAHT-sa*
language	язык (m)	*ya-ZEEK*
large	большой	*bahl'-SHOY*
larger	больше	*BOHL'-sh'yeh*
last	последний	*pahs-L'YEHD-nee*

late	поздно	*POHZ-na*
later	позже	*POHZ-zheh*
(to) laugh	смеяться	*smee-YAHT-sa*
laundry	прачечная (f)	*PRA-chehsh-na-ya*
law	закон (m)	*za-KOHN*
lawyer	юрист (m)	*yoo-REEST*
(to) learn	учить	*oo-CHEET'*
leather	кожа (f)	*KO-zha*
(to) leave (let)	оставлять	*ahs-tahv-L'YAHT'*
(to) leave (go by foot)	уходить	*oo-ha-DEET)*
left (direction)	левый	*L'YEH-vee*
leg	нога (f)	*na-GA*
lemon	лимон (m)	*lee-MOHN*
(to) lend	одолжить	*ah-dahl-ZHEET'*
less	меньше	*M'YEHN'-sheh*
lesson	урок (m)	*oo-ROHK*
(to) let (permit)	позволять	*pahz-va-L'YAHT'*
Let us...	Давайте...	*da-VAY-t'yeh...*
Let's go!	Пойдём!	*pa-ee-D'YOHM!*
letter (mail)	письмо (n)	*pees'-MO*
liberty	свобода (f)	*sva-BO-da*
license (sing.)	права (pl.)	*pra-VA*
lieutenant	лейтенант (n)	*lay-teh-NAHNT*
life	жизнь (f)	*zheez'n*
(to) lift	поднимать	*pahd-nee-MAHT'*
light	лёгкий	*L'YO-kee*
light (illumination)	свет (m)	*sv'yeht*
like	как	*kahk*
like this	так	*tahk*
(to) like	нравиться	*N'RA-veet-sa*
I like...	Мне нравится...	*mn'yeh NRA-veet-s'ya...*
lion	лев (m)	*l'yehf*
lips	губы	*GOO-bee*
lipstick	губная помада	*goob-NA-ya pa-MA-da*

(to) listen	слушать	*SLOO-shaht'*
little (small)	маленький	*MA-l'yen'-kee*
(a) little	немножко	*n'yehm-NOHZH-ka*
(to) live	жить	*zheet'*
living room	жилая комната	*zhee-LA-ya KOHM-na-ta*
lobby	передняя (f)	*peh-R'YED-n'ya-ya*
long	длинный	*DLEEN-nee*
(to) look	смотреть	*smaht-R'YEHT*
Look out!	Будьте	*BOOD-t'yeh*
	внимательны!	*vnee-MA-tehl-nee!*
(to) lose	терять	*t'yeh-R'YAHT'*
lost	потерянный	*pa-T'YEH-r'ya-nee*
lost and found office	бюро находок	*b'yoo-RO na-HO-dahk*
(a) lot	много	*MNO-ga*
(to) love	любить	*l'yoo-BEET'*
low	низкий	*NEEZ'-kee*
luck	удача (f)	*oo-DA-cha*
bad luck	неудача (f)	*n'yeh-oo-DA-cha*
Good luck!	Удачи!	*oo-DA-chee!*
luggage	багаж (m)	*ba-GAHZH*
lunch	обед (m)	*ah-B'YEHT*

M _____

machine	машина (f)	*ma-SHEE-na*
made in...	сделано в...	*SD'YEH-la-na v'...*
maid (servant)	горничная (f)	*GOHR-neech-na-ya*
mail	почта (f)	*POHCH-ta*
mailbox	почтовый ящик	*pahch-TOH-vee YAHSH-chik*
(to) make	делать	*D'YEH-laht'*
male (zoology)	самец (m)	*sa-M'YEHTS*
man	человек (m)	*cheh-la-V'YEK*
manager	менеджер (m)	*MEN-ne-jer*
(to) manufacture	производить	*pra-eez-va-DEET'*

many	много	*MNO-ga*
map	карта (f)	*KAR-ta*
March	март (n)	*mart*
market	рынок (m)	*REE-nahk*
married (m, f)	женатый (m)	*zheh-NA-tee*
	замужняя	*za-MOOZH-nee-ya* (f)
match (for fire)	спичка (f)	*SPEECH-ka*
material	материал (m)	*ma-t'yeh-R'YAHL*
What's the matter?	В чём дело?	*f ch'yohm D'YEH-la?*
May I?	Могу ли я?	*ma-GOO lee ya?*
May (month)	май (m)	*my*
maybe	может быть	*MO-zhet beet'*
me	меня	*men-YA*
to me	мне	*mn'yeh*
with me	со мной	*sa mnoy*
(to) mean	значить	*ZNA-cheet'*
meat	мясо (n)	*M'YA-sa*
mechanic	механик (m)	*meh-HA-neck*
medicine	медицина (f)	*meh-dee-TSEE-na*
to meet	встречать	*fstr-eh-CHAHT'*
Happy to meet you	очень рад	*OH-chehn raht*
member	член (m)	*ch'l'yen*
men (in sense of mankind, people)	люди (pl.)	*L'YOU-dee*
men's room	мужской туалет	*moozh-SKOY too-ah-L'YET*
(to) mend	чинить	*chee-NEET'*
menu	меню (n)	*meh-NEW*
message	записка (f)	*za-PEES-ka*
metal	металл (m)	*meh-TAHL*
meter	метр (m)	*m'yehtr*
middle	середина (f)	*seh-r'yeh-DEE-na*
in the middle	в середине	*v seh-r'yeh-DEE-n'yeh*
middle (adj.)	средний	*SRED-nee*

military	военный	*va-YEN-nee*
milk	молоко (n)	*ma-la-KO*
million	миллион (m)	*meel-YOHN*
mine (poss.)	мой	*moy*
mineral	минерал (m)	*mee-neh-RAHL*
minute	минута (f)	*mee-NOO-ta*
(to) miss (someone)	скучать	*skoo-CHAHT'*
(to) miss (a train)	пропустить	*pra-poos-TEET'*
mistake	ошибка (f)	*ah-SHEEB-ka*
misunderstanding	непонимание (n)	*n'yeh-pa-nee-MA-n'yeh*
model	модель (f)	*ma-DEHL'*
modern	современный	*sahv-r'yeh-MEHN-nee*
moment	момент (m)	*ma-M'YENT*
Monday	понедельник (m)	*pa-n'yeh-D'YEHL'-nik*
money (sing.)	деньги (pl.)	*D'YEHN'-gee*
monkey	обезьяна (f)	*ah-beh-Z'YA-na*
month	месяц (m)	*M'YEH-s'yahts*
monument	памятник (m)	*PA-m'yaht-nik*
moon	луна (f)	*loo-NA*
more	ещё	*yesh-CHO*
morning	утро (n)	*OOT-ra*
mosquito	комар (m)	*ka-MAR*
most	большинство (n)	*bahl'-shinst-VO*
mostly	в большинстве	*v bahl'-shinst-V'YEH*
mother	мать (f)	*maht'*
motor	мотор (m)	*ma-TOR*
motorcycle	мотоцикл (m)	*ma-ta-TSEEKL*
mountains	гора (f)	*ga-RA* (s.)
	горы (pl.)	*goh-REE (pl.)*
mouse	мышь (f)	*mweesh*
mouth	рот (m)	*roht*
movies	кино (n)	*kee-NO*
much	много	*MNO-ga*
museum	музей (m)	*moo-Z'YEY*

| mushrooms | грибы (pl.) | *gree-BWEE* |
| music | музыка (f) | *MOO-zee-ka* |

N _____

name	имя (n)	*EEM-ya*
napkin	салфетка (f)	*sahl-F'YET-ka*
narrow	узкий	*OOZ-kee*
near	близко	*BLEES-ka*
necessary	необходимо	*n'yeh-ab-ha-DEE-ma*
neck	шея (f)	*SHEH-ya*
necktie	галстук (m)	*GAHL-stook*
I need	мне нужно	*mn'yeh NOOZH-na*
we need	нам нужно	*nahm NOOZH-na*
neighborhood	соседство (n)	*sa-s'YET-stva*
nervous	нервный	*NEHR-vnee*
net weight	чистый вес	*CHEE-stee v'yes*
never	никогда	*nee-kahg-DA*
Never mind!	Ничего!	*nee-cheh-VO!*
new	новый	*NO-vee*
news	новости (pl.)	*NO-va-stee*
newspaper	газета (f)	*ga-Z'YEH-ta*
next	следующий	*SL'YEH-doosh-chee*
nice	приятный	*pree-YAHT-nee*
night	ночь (f)	*nohch*
nightgown	халат (m)	*ha-LAHT*
nine	девять	*D'YEH-v'yaht*
nineteen	девятнадцать	*d'yeh-v'yaht-NAHT-tsaht*
ninety	девяносто	*d'yeh-v'ya-NO-sta*
no	нет	*n'yet*
nobody	никто	*neek-TOH*
noise	шум (m)	*shoom*
noon	полдень (m)	*POHL-d'yen'*
north	север (m)	*S'YEH-vehr*
nose	нос (m)	*nohs*

not	не	n'yeh
not any	ни один	nee ah-DEEN
not yet	ещё нет	yesh-CHO n'yet
nothing	ничего	nee-cheh-VO
nothing at all	совсем ничего	sahf-S'YEM nee-cheh-VO
November	Ноябрь	na-YAHBR'
now	сейчас	s'yey-CHAS
nowhere	никуда	nee-koo-DA
number	номер	NO-mehr

O _____

occasionally	случайно	sloo-CHAI-na
occupied	занятый	ZAHN-ya-tee
ocean	океан (m)	ah-keh-AHN
October	Октябрь	ahk-T'YABR'
(to) offer	предлагать	pred-la-GAHT'
office	офис (m)	OH-fees
officer	офицер (m)	ah-fee-TSER
official	официальный	ah-fee-TSAHL'nee
often	часто	CHA-sta
oil	масло (n)	MA-sla
O.K.	хорошо	ha-ra-SHO
old	старый	STA-ree
on	на	na
on time	вовремя	VO-vrem-ya
once	однажды	ahd-NAHZH-dee
At once!	Сейчас же!	s'yey-CHAHS zheh!
one only	только один	tohl'ka ah-DEEN
open	открыто	aht-KREE-ta
(to) open	открывать	aht-kree-VAHT'
opera	опера (f)	OH-peh-ra
opinion	мнение (n)	mn'YEH-nee-yeh
opportunity	возможность (f)	vahz-MOHZH-nast'
opposite	напротив	na-PROH-teef

or	или	*EE-lee*
orange (fruit)	апельсин	*ah-p'yel'-SEEN*
orchestra	оркестр (m)	*or-KESS-tr'*
order (comm.)	заказ (m)	*za-KAHS*
(to) order (comm.)	заказывать	*za-KA-zee-vaht'*
in order to	чтобы	*sh'to-bee*
original	оригинальный	*ah-ree-ghee-NAHL'-nee*
other	другой	*droo-GOY*
You ought to...	Вы должны...	*vwee dahl-ZHNEE...*
our	наш (m), наша (f), наше (n)	*nahsh, NA-sha, NA-sheh*
out of...	из...	*eez...*
outside	снаружи	*sna-ROO-zhee*
over	через	*CHEH-rez*
(to) owe	быть должным	*beet DOHLZH-neem*
(to) own	владеть	*vla-D'YEHT'*
owner	владелец (m)	*vla-D'YEH-l'yehts*
ox	вол (m)	*vohl*

P _____

(to) pack	паковать	*pa-ka-VAHT'*
package	упаковка (f)	*oo-pa-KOHV-ka*
paid	оплачено	*ah-PLA-cheh-na*
pain	боль (f)	*bohl'*
(to) paint	красить	*KRA-seet'*
painting	картина (f)	*kar-TEE-na*
palace	дворец (m)	*dva-R'YETS*
pants	брюки (pl.)	*BR'YOO-kee*
paper	бумага (f)	*boo-MA-ga*
parade	парад (m)	*pa-RAHT*
Pardon me!	Извините меня!	*eez-vee-NEE-t'yeh men-YA!*
parents	родители (pl.)	*ra-DEE-t'yeh-lee*
(to) park	парковаться	*par-ka-VAHT-s'ya*

park	парк (m)	*park*
part	часть (f)	*chahst'*
partner	партнёр	*part-N'YOR*
passenger	пассажир (m)	*pah-sa-ZHEER*
passport	паспорт (m)	*PAHS-port*
(to) pay	платить	*pla-TEET'*
peace	мир (m)	*meer*
pen	ручка (f)	*ROOCH-ka*
pencil	карандаш (m)	*ka-rahn-DAHSH*
people	люди (pl.)	*L'YOO-dee*
pepper	перец (m)	*P'YEH-r'yehts*
percent	процент (m)	*pra-TSENT*
perfect	отличный	*aht-LEECH-nee*
perfume	духи	*doo-HEE*
perhaps	возможно	*vahz-MOHZH-na*
permit	разрешение (n)	*rahz-reh-SHE-nee-yeh*
permitted	разрешено	*rahz-r'yeh-sheh-NO*
person	человек (m)	*cheh-la-VEK*
photograph	фотография (f)	*fo-ta-GRA-fee-ya*
piano	пианино (n)	*pee-ah-NEE-no*
picture	картина (f)	*kar-TEE-na*
piece	кусок (m)	*koo-SOK*
pigeon	голубь (m)	*GO-loop'*
pill	таблетка (f)	*tahb-L'YET-ka*
pillow	подушка (f)	*pa-DOOSH-ka*
pin	булавка (f)	*boo-LAHF-ka*
pink	розовый	*RO-zo-vee*
place	место (n)	*M'YES-ta*
plan	план (m)	*plahn*
plane (airplane)	самолёт (m)	*sa-ma-L'YOHT*
planet	планета (f)	*pla-N'YEH-ta*
plant (garden)	растение (n)	*ra-ST'YEH-nee-yeh*
plant (factory)	завод (m)	*za-VOHT*
plate	тарелка (f)	*ta-R'YEL-ka*
(to) play	играть	*ee-GRAHT'*
pleasant	приятный	*pree-YAHT-nee*

Please!	Пожалуйста!	*pa-ZHAH-loo-sta!*
pleasure	удовольствие (n)	*oo-da-VOL'ST-vee-yeh*
pocket	карман (m)	*kar-MAHN*
poem	поэма (f)	*po-EH-ma*
Poland	Польша	*POHL'-sha*
Pole (m, f)	поляк (m)	*pahl'-YAHK*
Pole (f)	полячка (f)	*pahl'-YACH-ka*
police	милиция	*mee-LEE-tsee-ya*
Polish	польский	*POHL'-skee*
polite	вежливый	*VEZH-lee-vee*
politics	политика (f)	*pa-LEE-tee-ka*
poor	бедный	*B'YED-nee*
popular	популярный	*pa-poo-L'YAR-nee*
pork	свинина (f)	*svee-NEE-na*
port	порт (m)	*port*
possible	возможно	*vahz-MO-zhna*
postcard	открытка (f)	*aht-KREET-ka*
post office	почта (f)	*POHCH-ta*
potato	картошка (f)	*kar-TOSH-ka*
(to) practice	практиковаться	*prahk-tee-ka-VAHT-s'ya*
(to) prefer	предпочитать	*pret-pa-chee-TAHT'*
pregnancy	беременность (f)	*beh-REH-men-nohst'*
(to) prepare	приготовить	*pree-ga-TOH-veet'*
at present	в настоящее время	*v na-sta-YA-sh'che-ye VR'YEHM'-ya*
president	президент (m)	*preh-zee-D'YENT*
(to) press (clothes)	гладить	*GLA-deet'*
pretty	симпатичный	*seem-pa-TEECH-nee*
price	цена (f)	*tzeh-NA*
priest	священник (m)	*sv'ya-SH'CHEN-neek*
prison	тюрьма (f)	*t'yoor'-MA*
private	частный	*CHAHST-nee*
probably	возможно	*vahz-MOHZH-na*
problem	проблема (f)	*pra-BL'YEH-ma*
production	производство (n)	*pra-eez-VOHT-stva*

profession	профессия (f)	*pra-F'YES-see-ya*
professor	профессор (m)	*pra-FES-sor*
profit	прибыль (f)	*PREE-beel'*
program	программа (f)	*pra-GRAHM-ma*
(to) promise	обещать	*ah-b'yeh-SHCHAHT'*
pronunciation	произношение (n)	*pra-eez-na-SHEH-nee-yeh*
propaganda	пропаганда (f)	*pra-pa-GAHN-da*
property	владение (n)	*vla-D'YEH-nee-yeh*
public	публика (f)	*POOB-lee-ka*
(to) publish	издавать	*eez-da-VAHT'*
publisher	издатель (m)	*eez-DA-t'yel'*
(to) pull	тянуть	*T'YA-noot'*
purse	сумка (f)	*SOOM-ka*
(to) push	толкать	*tahl-KAT'*
I put	Я кладу	*(ya) kla-DOO*
you put	Вы кладёте	*(vwee) kla-D'YO-t'yeh*

Q ———————————————

quality	качество (n)	*KA-chest-va*
quarrel	ссора (f)	*SSO-ra*
queen	королева (f)	*ka-ra-L'YEH-va*
question	вопрос (m)	*va-PROHS*
quickly	быстро	*BEE-stra*
quiet	спокойно	*spa-KOY-na*
quite	совершенно	*sa-ver-SHEN-na*

R ———————————————

rabbit	кролик (m)	*KRO-lik*
race (contest)	гонка (f)	*GOHN-ka*
radio	радио (n)	*RA-deeo*
railroad	железная дорога	*zheh-L'YEZ-na-ya da-RO-ga*
raincoat	плащ (m)	*plahsh'ch*

It's raining	Идёт дождь	ee-D'YOHT doshd'
rarely	редко	R'YET-ka
rat	крыса (f)	KREE-sa
rate (of exchange)	курс (m)	koorss
razor	лезвие (n)	LEZ-vee-yeh
(to) read	читать	chee-TAHT
ready (finished)	готовый	ga-TOH-vee
real	реальный	reh-AHL'-nee
receipt	чек (m)	chek
(to) receive	получать	pa-loo-CHAHT
recently	недавно	n'yeh-DA-vna
(to) recognize	узнавать	oo-zna-VAHT
(to) recommend	рекомендовать	reh-ka-men-dah-VAHT
red	красный	KRA-snee
refrigerator	холодильник (m)	ha-la-DEEL'-nik
(to) refuse	отказать	aht-ka-ZAHT
My regards to...	Мой привет...	...moy pree-V'YET
regular	обычный	ah-BEECH-nee
religion	религия	reh-LEE-ghee-ya
(to) remain	оставаться	ah-sta-VAHT-s'ya
(to) remember	помнить	POHM-neet'
(to) rent	снимать	snee-MAHT
(to) repair	ремонтировать	reh-mahn-TEE-ra-vaht'
(to) repeat	повторять	pa-f'tah-R'YAHT
report	доклад (m)	dah-KLAHT
(to) represent	представлять	pr'yet-stav-L'YAHT
representative	представитель (m)	prehd-sta-VEE-t'yel'
responsible	ответственный	aht-V'YETST-veh-nee
(the) rest	отдых (m)	OHT-dikh
(to) rest	отдыхать	ahd-dee-HAHT
restaurant	ресторан	res-ta-RAHN
(to) restrict	ограничивать	ah-gra-NEE-chee-vaht'
(to) return	вернуться	ver-NOOT-sa
revolution	революция	reh-va-L'YOO-tsee-ya

reward	награда (f)	na-GRA-da
rich	богатый	ba-GA-tee
(to) ride (a horse)	ездить верхом	YEZ-deet' vehr-HOHM
(to) ride (in a vehicle)	ездить	YEZ-deet'
rifle	винтовка	veen-TOHF-ka
right (correct)	правильно	PRA-veel'-na
right (direction)	направо	na-PRA-va
Right away!	Сразу!	SRA-zoo!
ring	кольцо (n)	kahl'-TSO
riot	восстание (n)	vah-STA-nee-yeh
river	река (f)	r'yeh-KA
road	дорога (f)	da-RO-ga
roof	крыша (f)	KREE-sha
room	комната (f)	KOHM-na-ta
route	маршрут (m)	marsh-ROOT
rug	ковёр (m)	ka-V'YOR
(to) run	бежать	bee-ZHAHT'
Russia	Россия	ra-SEE-ya
Russian (m, f)	русский (m)	ROO-skee
	русская (f)	ROO-ska-ya

S

sad	печальный	peh-chahl'-nee
safely	безопасно	b'yeh-za-PA-sna
sailor	моряк (m)	mah-R'YAHK
saint	святой (m)	sv'ya-TOY
salad	салат (m)	sa-LAHT
salary	зарплата (f)	zar-PLA-ta
salt	соль (f)	sohl'
same	тот же самый	toht zhe SA-mee
sand	песок (m)	p'yeh-SOCK
sandwich	бутерброд (m)	boo-ter-BROHT

Saturday	суббота (f)	*soo-BO-ta*
sausage	колбаса (f)	*kahl-ba-SA*
(to) say	говорить	*ga-va-REET'*
scarf	шарф (m)	*sharf*
school	школа (f)	*SHKO-la*
science	наука (f)	*na-OO-ka*
scientist	ученый (m)	*oo-CHO-nee*
scissors	ножницы (pl.)	*NOHZH-nee-tsee*
sea	море (n)	*MO-r'yeh*
season	сезон (m)	*seh-ZOHN*
seat	место (n)	*M'YES-ta*
secretary	секретарь (m)	*seh-kreh-TAR'*
	секретарша (f)	*seh-kreh-TAR-sha*
(to) see	видеть	*VEE-d'yeht'*
seldom	редко	*R'YET-ka*
(to) sell	продавать	*pra-da-VAHT'*
(to) send	посылать	*pa-see-LAHT'*
(to) separate	разделять	*rahz-d'yeh-l'YAHT'*
September	сентябрь (m)	*sen-T'YABR'*
serious	серьёзный	*s'yer-YOHZ-nee*
service (hotel, restaurant)	служба (f)	*SLOOZH-ba*
seven	семь	*s'yem*
seventeen	семнадцать	*s'yem-NAHT-tsaht'*
seventy	семьдесят	*S'YEM-d'yeh-S'YAHT*
several	несколько	*N'YEH-skahl'-ka*
sharp	острый	*OH-stree*
shave	бритьё	*bree-T'YO*
she	она	*ah-NA*
sheep	овца	*ahf-TSA*
ship	корабль (m)	*ka-RAHBL'*
(to) ship (merchandise)	посылать	*pa-see-LAHT'*
shirt	рубашка (f)	*roo-BA-shka*
shoe	ботинок (m)	*ba-TEE-nok*
shop	магазин (m)	*ma-ga-ZEEN*

short	короткий	*ka-ROHT-kee*
shoulder	плечо (n)	*pl'ye-CHO*
(to) show	показывать	*pa-KA-zee-vaht'*
Show me!	Покажите мне!	*pa-ka-ZHEE-t'yeh mn'yeh!*
shower	душ (m)	*doosh*
(to) shut	закрывать	*za-kree-VAHT'*
sick	больной	*bahl'-NOY*
sign	знак (m)	*znahk*
silk	шелк (m)	*sholk*
silver	серебро (n)	*s'yeh-r'yeh-BRO*
simple	простой	*pra-STOY*
sincere	честный	*CHEST-nee*
(to) sing	петь	*p'yet'*
singer	певец (m)	*pee-V'YETS*
sister	сестра (f)	*s'yeh-STRA*
(to) sit	сидеть	*see-D'YET'*
Sit down!	Садитесь!	*sa-DEET-yes'!*
six	шесть	*shest*
sixteen	шестнадцать	*shest-NAHT-t'saht'*
sixty	шестьдесят	*shess-d'yeh-S'YAHT*
size	размер (m)	*rahz-M'YEHR*
skin	кожа (f)	*KO-zha*
skirt	юбка (f)	*YOOP-ka*
sky	небо (n)	*N'YEH-ba*
(to) sleep	спать	*spaht'*
slowly	медленно	*M'YED-len-na*
small	маленький	*MA-l'yen'-kee*
smell	запах (m)	*ZA-pahkh*
(to) smoke	курить	*koo-REET'*
snow	снег (m)	*sn'yek*
so	так	*tahk*
soap	мыло (n)	*MEE-la*
socks	носки (pl.)	*na-SKEE*
soft	мягкий	*M'YAKH-kee*
soldier	солдат (m)	*sahl-DAHT*
some (a little)	немного	*n'yeh-MNO-ga*

somebody	кто-нибудь	K'TOH-nee-boot'
something	что-нибудь	SHTOH-nee-boot'
sometimes	иногда	ee-nahg-DA
somewhere	где-нибудь	G'D'YEH-nee-boot'
son	сын (m)	sin
song	песня (f)	P'YES-n'ya
soon	скоро	SCORE-ah
(I am) sorry	Я сожалею	ya sa-zha-L'EH-yoo
soup	суп (m)	soup
south	юг (m)	yuke
South America	Южная Америка	YOOZH-na-ya ah-MEH-ree-ka
South American	южноамериканский	YOOZH-na ah-meh-ree-KAHN-skee
Spain	Испания	ee-SPA-nee-ya
Spaniard (m, f)	испанец	ee-SPA-n'yets
	испанка (f)	ee-SPAHN-ka
Spanish	испанский	ee-SPAHN-skee
(to) speak	говорить	ga-va-REET'
special	специальный	spetz-YAHL-nee
(to) spend	тратить	TRA-teet'
spoon	ложка (f)	LOZH-ka
sport	спорт (m)	sport
spring	весна (f)	vehss-NA
stairs	лестница (f)	L'YES-neet-sa
stamp (postage)	марка (f)	MAR-ka
star	звезда (f)	zv'yez-DA
(to) start	начинать	na-chee-NAHT'
steak	бифштекс (m)	beef-SHTEKS
station (train)	станция (f)	STAHN-tsee-ya
(to) stay	оставаться	ah-sta-VAHT-s'ya
steel	сталь (f)	stahl
stomach	желудок (m)	zheh-LOO-dahk
stone	камень (m)	KA-mehn'
Stop!	Остановитесь!	ah-sta-na-VEE-t'yes!
(a) stop (bus, etc.)	остановка (f)	ah-sta-NOV-ka

store	магазин (m)	*ma-ga-ZEEN*
storm	буря (f)	*BOO-r'ya*
(a) story	рассказ (m)	*rahs-KAHS*
Straight ahead!	Прямо!	*PR'YA-ma!*
strange	странный	*STRA-nee*
street	улица (f)	*OO-leet-sa*
strong	сильный	*SEEL'-nee*
student	студент (m)	*stoo-D'YENT*
	студентка (f)	*stoo-D'YENT-ka*
(to) study	изучать	*ee-zoo-CHAHT'*
style	стиль (m)	*steel'*
subway	метро (n)	*meh-TRO*
success	успех (m)	*oo-SPEHKH*
such	такой	*ta-KOY*
suddenly	вдруг	*v'drook*
sugar	сахар (m)	*SA-har*
suit (clothes)	костюм (m)	*ka-ST'YOOM*
suitcase	чемодан (m)	*cheh-ma-DAHN*
summer	лето (n)	*L'YEH-ta*
sun	солнце (n)	*SOHN-tseh*
Sunday	воскресенье (n)	*va-skreh-S'YEH-nee-yeh*
sure	верно	*V'YEHR-na*
surprise	удивление (n)	*oo-deev-L'YEH-nee-yeh*
Swede (m, f)	швед (m)	*shv'yet*
	шведка (f)	*shv'YET-ka*
Sweden	Швеция	*SHVEH-tsee-ya*
Swedish	шведский	*sh-VEHT-skee*
sweet	сладкий	*SLAHT-kee*
(to) swim	плавать	*PLA-vaht'*
swimming pool	бассейн	*ba-SAYN*

T _____

| table | стол (m) | *stohl* |
| tailor | портной (m) | *part-NOY* |

(to) take	брать	*braht'*
(to) talk	разговаривать	*rahz-ga-VA-ree-vaht'*
tall	высокий	*vwee-SO-kee*
tape	плёнка (f)	*PL'YOHN-ka*
tape recorder	магнитофон (m)	*mahg-nee-ta-FOHN*
Tartar	татарин (n)	*ta-TA-reen*
	татарский (adj.)	*ta-TAHR-skee*
tax	налог (m)	*na-LOHK*
taxi	такси (n)	*tahk-SEE*
tea	чай (m)	*chy*
(to) teach	учить	*oo-CHEET'*
teacher (m, f)	учитель (m)	*oo-CHEET-yel'*
	учительница (f)	*oo-CHEET-yel'-nee-tsa*
team	команда (f)	*ka-MAHN-da*
telegram	телеграмма (f)	*teh-leh-GRA-ma*
telephone	телефон (m)	*teh-leh-FOHN*
television	телевидение (n)	*teh-leh-VEE-dee-nee-yeh*
(to) tell	сказать	*ska-ZAHT'*
Tell her	скажите ей	*ska-ZHEET-yeh yay*
Tell him	скажите ему	*ska-ZHEET-yeh yeh-MOO*
Tell me	скажите мне	*ska-ZHEET-yeh mn'yeh*
temperature	температура (f)	*t'yem-peh-ra-TOO-ra*
ten	десять	*D'YEH-s'yaht*
terrible	ужасный	*oo-ZHAHS-nee*
than	чем	*chem*
(to) thank	благодарить	*bla-ga-da-REET'*
Thank you!	Спасибо!	*spa-SEE-ba!*
that (one)	тот	*toht*
that (dem.)	тот (m), та (f), то (n)	*toht, tah, toh*
that (rel.)	который (m), которая (f), которое (n)	*ka-TO-ree, ka-TO-ra-ya, ka-TO-ra-yeh*
theater	театр (m)	*tee-AHTR*
their, them, to them	их	*eekh*

then	тогда	*tahg-DA*
there	там	*tahm*
therefore	поэтому	*pa-EH-ta-moo*
these	эти	*EH-tee*
they	они	*ah-NEE*
thin	тонкий	*TOHN-kee*
thing	вещь (f)	*v'yesh'ch*
(to) think	думать	*DOO-maht'*
I think that...	Я думаю, что...	*ya DOO-ma-yoo shtoh...*
What do you think?	Как вы думаете?	*kahk vwee DOO-ma-ye-t'yeh?*
third	третий	*TR'YEH-tee*
thirsty (to want to drink)	хотеть пить	*ha-T'YEHT peet'*
thirteen	тринадцать	*tree-NAHT-saht'*
thirty	тридцать	*TREET-saht'*
this	это	*EH-ta*
those	те	*t'yeh*
thousand	тысяча	*TEE-seh-cha*
three	три	*tree*
throat	горло (n)	*GOR-la*
through	до конца	*da kahn-TSA*
Thursday	четверг (m)	*chet-V'YERK*
tie	галстук (m)	*GAHL-stook*
tiger	тигр (m)	*teegr*
time	время (n)	*VR'YEH-m'yah*
tip	чаевые (pl.)	*cha-yeh-VEE-yeh*
tire (auto)	шина (f)	*SHEE-na*
(to be) tired	устал (m), устала (f)	*oo-STAHL (m), oo-STA-la (f)*
to (direction)	к, ко	*k', ka*
to (in order to)	чтобы	*SHTO-bee*
today	сегодня	*s'yeh-VOHD-n'ya*
together	вместе	*vm'YEHST-yeh*
toilet	туалет (m)	*twa-LET*
tomorrow	завтра	*ZAHF-tra*

tomorrow morning	завтра утром	*ZAHF-tra OO-trahm*
tomorrow night	завтра вечером	*ZAHF-tra V'YEH-cheh-rahm*
tonight	сегодня вечером	*s'yeh-VOHD-n'ya V'YEH-cheh-rahm*
too (also)	тоже	*TOH-zheh*
too (excessive)	слишком	*S'LEESH-kahm*
tooth	зуб (m)	*zoop*
toothbrush	зубная щётка (f)	*zoob-NA-ya SH'CHOT-ka*
toothpaste	зубная паста (f)	*zoob-NA-ya PA-sta*
tour	поездка (f)	*pa-YEZD-ka*
towel	полотенце (n)	*pa-la-T'YEN-tseh*
tower	башня (f)	*BAHSH-n'ya*
town	город (m)	*GO-raht*
toy	игрушка (f)	*ee-GROOSH-ka*
trade fair	торговая выставка (f)	*tar-GO-va-ya VEE-stahf-ka*
traffic	движение (n)	*dvee-ZHEH-nee-yeh*
train	поезд (m)	*PO-yest*
translation	перевод (m)	*peh-r'yeh-VOHT*
(to) travel	путешествовать	*poo-teh-SHEST-va-vaht'*
travel agency	туристическое агентство (n)	*too-ristee-CHES-ka-yeh ah-GHENST-va*
traveler	путешественник (m)	*poo-teh-SHEST-ven-nik*
treasurer	казначей (m)	*kahz-na-CHAY*
tree	дерево (n)	*d'YEH-r'yeh-va*
trip	путешествие (n)	*poo-teh-SHEST-vee-yeh*
trouble	беспокойство (n)	*b'yes-pa-KOY-stva*
truck	грузовик (m)	*groo-za-VEEK*
truth	правда (f)	*PRAHV-da*
(to) try (attempt)	пробовать	*PRO-ba-vaht'*
Tuesday	вторник (m)	*F'TOR-nik*
tunnel	туннель (m)	*too-NEHL'*
Turkey	Турция	*TOOR-tsee-ya*

Turkish (adj.)	турецкий	*too-RETS-kee*
Turk (m, f)	турок (m)	*TOO-rahk*
	турчанка (f)	*toor-CHAHN-ka*
(to) turn off	выключать	*vwee-kl'yoo-CHAHT'*
(to) turn on	включать	*f'kl'yoo-CHAHT'*
twelve	двенадцать	*dvee-NAHT-saht'*
twenty	двадцать	*DVA-tsaht'*
two	два	*dva*
typewriter	пишущая машинка	*PEE-shoosh-cha-ya ma-SHEEN-ka*
typist (m, f)	машинист (m)	*ma-shee-NEEST*
	машинистка (f)	*ma-shee-NEEST-ka*

U ———————————————————————

ugly	уродливый	*oo-ROHD-lee-vee*
Ukraine	Украина	*oo-kra-EE-na*
Ukrainian (m, f)	украинец (m)	*oo-kra-EE-n'yets*
	украинка (f)	*oo-kra-EEN-ka*
umbrella	зонтик	*ZOHN-teek*
uncultured	некультурный	*n'yeh-kool'-TOOR-nee*
under	под	*poht*
(to) understand	понимать	*pa-nee-MAHT'*
Do you understand?	Вы понимаете?	*vwee pa-nee-MA-yeh-t'yeh?*
I don't understand	Я не понимаю	*ya n'yeh pa-nee-MA-yoo.*
underwear	нижнее бельё (n)	*neezh-neh-yeh bee-L'YOH*
unfortunately	к сожалению	*k' sap-zhahl-YEH-nee-yoo*
uniform	униформа (f)	*oo-nee-FOR-ma*
union	союз (m)	*sa-YOOS*
United Nations	Объединенные Нации	*ahb-yeh-dee-N'YOHN-nee-yeh NAH-tsee*

United States	Соединенные Штаты	*sa-yeh-deen-YO-nee-yeh SH'TA-tee*
USSR	Советский Союз (m)	*sa-V'YET-skee sa-YOOS*
university	университет (m)	*oo-nee-veer-see T'YEHT*
unlawful	незаконный	*n'yeh-za-KOHN-nee*
until	до	*da*
up	вверх	*v'verkh*
urgent	срочный	*S'ROHCH-nee*
us, to us	нас, нам	*nahs, nahm*
(to) use	использовать	*eez-POHL-za-vaht'*
used to (in the habit of)	привычный	*pree-VEECH-nee*
useful	полезный	*pa-L'YEZ-nee*
usual	обычный	*ah-BEECH-nee*

V _____

vacant	свободный	*sva-BOHD-nee*
vacation	каникулы (pl.)	*ka-NEE-koo-lee*
vaccination	прививка (f)	*pree-VEEF-ka*
valley	равнина (f)	*rahv-NEE-na*
value	ценность	*TSEHN-nost'*
various	различный	*raz-LEECH-nee*
vegetables	овощи	*OH-va-sh'chee*
very	очень	*OH-chen'*
very well	очень хорошо	*OH-chen' ha-ra-SHO*
view	вид (m)	*veet*
village	деревня (f)	*d'yeh-R'YEV-n'ya*
violin	скрипка (f)	*SKR'EEP-ka*
(to) visit	посещать	*pa-s'yeh-SH'CHAT'*
voice	голос (m)	*GO-lahs*
Volga	Волга (f)	*VOHL-ga*
voyage	путешествие	*poo-te-SHEST-vee-eh*

W _____

(to) wait	ждать	*zh'daht*
waiter	официант (m)	*ah-fee-tsee-AHNT*
waitress	официантка (f)	*ah-fee-tsee-AHNT-ka*
(to) walk	идти пешком	*eet-TEE p'yesh-KOM*
wall	стена (f)	*steh-NA*
wallet	бумажник (m)	*boo-MAHZH-nik*
(to) want	хотеть	*ha-T'YET'*
I want	Я хочу	*ya ha-CHOO*
he (she) wants	он (она) хочет	*ohn (ah-NA) HO-chet*
you (we, they) want	вы хотите, мы хотим, они хотят	*vwee ha-TEET-yeh, mwee ha-TEEM, ah-NEE ha-T'YAHT*
Do you want...?	Вы хотите...?	*Vwee ha-TEET-yee...?*
war	война (f)	*voy-NA*
warm	теплый	*T'YOP-lee*
(I, he, she, it) was	Я был, он был, она была, оно было	*ya bweel, ohn bweel, ah-NA bwee-LA, ah-NO BWEE-la*
(to) wash	мыть	*mweet'*
watch	часы (pl.)	*cha-SEE*
(to) watch	смотреть	*sma-TR'YET'*
Watch out!	Будьте внимательны!	*BOOT-tyeh vnee-MA-tel-nee!*
water	вода (f)	*va-DA*
way	путь (m)	*poot'*
we	мы	*mwee*
weak	слабый	*SLA-bee*
(to) wear	носить	*na-SEET'*
weather	погода (f)	*pa-GO-da*
wedding	свадьба (f)	*SVAHD'-ba*
Wednesday	среда (f)	*sreh-DA*
week	неделя (f)	*neh-D'YEH-l'ya*

weight	вес (m)	*v'yes*
Welcome!	Добро пожаловать!	*DOH-bro pa-ZHA-lo-vaht'!*
You are welcome!	Пожалуйста!	*pa-ZHAHL-sta!*
well	хорошо	*ha-ra-SHO*
he (she, it) went	он ушёл, (она ушла), (это ушло)	*ohn oo-SHOLL, (ah-NA oo-SHLA), (EH-ta oo-SHLO)*
you (we, they) went	вы (мы, они) ушли	*vwee (mwee, ah-NEE) oo-SHLEE*
you (we, they) were	вы (мы, они) были	*vwee (mwee, ah-NEE) BWEE-lee*
west	запад (m)	*ZA-paht*
what	что	*shtoh*
What's the matter?	В чём дело?	*f' ch'yom D'YEH-la?*
What time is it?	Который час?	*ka-TOH-ree chahs?*
At what time?	В котором часу?	*f'ka-TOH-rahm chahs-SOO?*
when?	когда?	*kahg-DA?*
where?	куда?	*koo-DA?*
whether	ли	*lee*
which	который (m)	*ka-TOH-ree*
while	пока	*pa-KA*
white	белый	*B'YEH-lee*
who?	кто?	*k'toh?*
whole	целый	*TSEH-lee*
whom?	кого?	*ka-VO*
whose?	чей?	*chay?*
why?	почему?	*pa-cheh-MOO?*
wide	широкий	*shee-RO-kee*
widow	вдова (f)	*v'da-VA*
widower	вдовец (m)	*v'da-v'YETS*
wife	жена (f)	*zheh-NA*
wild	дикий	*DEE-kee*

will (shall)		
I will	Я буду	*ya BOO-do*
he (she, it) will	он (она, оно) будет	*ohn (ah-NA, ah-NO) bood'yet*
you (we, they) will	вы будете, мы) будем, (они) будут	*vwee BOOD-yet-t'yeh (mwee BOOD-d'yem) (ah-NEE BOO-doot)*
(to) win	выигрывать	*vwee-EE-gree-vaht'*
wind	ветер (m)	*V'YEH-ter*
window	окно (n)	*ahk-NO*
wine	вино (n)	*vee-NO*
winner	победитель (m)	*pa-b'yeh-DEE-t'yehl'*
winter	зима (f)	*zee-MA*
wish	желание (n)	*zheh-LA-nee-yeh*
(to) wish	желать	*zheh-LAHT'*
without	без	*b'yes*
with	с	*s*
wolf	волк (m)	*vohlk*
woman	женщина (f)	*ZHENSH-chee-na*
wonderful	прекрасный	*preh-KRA-snee*
wood	дерево (n)	*D'YEH-r'yeh-va*
wool	шерсть (f)	*sherst'*
word	слово (n)	*SLO-va*
work	работа (f)	*rah-BO-ta*
(to) work	работать	*rah-BO-taht*
world	мир (m)	*meer*
worry	волноваться	*vahl-na-VAHT-s'ya*
Don't worry!	Не волнуйтесь!	*n'yeh vahl-NOO-yeh-t'yes!*
worse	хуже	*HOO-zheh*
would	...бы... (before or after verb)	*...bwee...*
Would you like...?	Хотите ли вы...?	*ha-TEET-yeh lee vwee...?*
I would like...	Я хотел бы...	*ya ha-T'YEL bwee...*
(to) write	писать	*pee-SAHT'*
Write it!	Напишите это!	*na-pee-SHEE-t'yeh EH-ta!*

| writer | писатель (m) | *pee-SA-t'yel* |
| wrong | неправильно | *n'yeh-PRA-veel-na* |

X _____

| X-ray | рентген (m) | *r'yent-GHEN* |

Y _____

year	год (m)	*goht*
yellow	жёлтый	*ZH'YOL-tee*
yes	да	*da*
yesterday	вчера	*f'cheh-RA*
yet	ещё	*yesh-CHO*
you (sing.)	ты (sing.)	*tee*
you (pl.)	вы (pl.)	*vwee*
young	молодой	*ma-la-DOY*
your	ваш	*vahsh*
Yugoslavia	Югославия	*yoo-ga-SLAH-vee-ya*
Yugoslavian (m, f)	югослав	*yoo-ga-SLAHF*
	югославка (f)	*yoo-ga-SLAHF-ka*

Z _____

zebra	зебра (f)	*ZEH-bra*
zero	ноль (m)	*nohl'*
zipper	молния (f)	*MOHL-nee-ya*
zone	зона (f)	*ZO-na*
zoo	зоопарк (m)	*zo-oh-PARK*

Point to the Answer

This final Point to the Answer, placed at the end of the Dictionary section, will enable you to elicit responses to many short questions you may form from the Dictionary.

Укажите, пожалуйста, ваш ответ на мой вопрос на следующей странице. Большое спасибо.

Да.	Нет.	Возможно.	Позже.	Сейчас же.
Yes	No.	Perhaps.	Later.	At once.

Конечно.	Хорошо.	Извините.
Certainly.	All right.	Excuse me.

Я понимаю.	Я не понимаю.
I understand.	I don't understand.

Что вы хоттите?	Я знаю.	Я не знаю.
What do you want?	I know.	I don't know.

Открыто.	Закрыто.
Open.	Closed.

Слишком много.	Недостаточно.
Too much.	Not enough.

Не входить.	Запрещено.
No admittance.	It is forbidden.

Договорились.	Очень хорошо.	Это не хорошо.
It is agreed.	Very good.	It isn't good.

Это близко.
It's near.

Слишком далеко.
Too far.

Очень далеко.
Very far.

Поверните налево!
Turn left!

Поверните направо!
Turn right!

Идите прямо!
Go straight ahead!

Идёмте со мной!
Come with me!

Подождите меня.
Wait for me.

Я должен идти.
I must go.

Приходите позже.
Come back later.

Я скоро вернусь.
I'll be right back.

Меня зовут _____.
My name is _____.

Ваше имя? Фамилия?
Your first name? last name?

Номер телефона?
Telephone number?

Адрес?
Address?

Signet

A World of Reference at Your Fingertips

THE NEW ROBERT'S RULES OF ORDER (2ND EDITION)
MARY A. DE VRIES
Long considered the bible of parliamentary procedures, this new edition updates the archaic prose of the original into easy-to-follow, contemporary English while maintaining the work's original order and content.

THE NEW AMERICAN ROGET'S COLLEGE THESAURUS IN DICTIONARY FORM (REVISED & COMPLETELY UPDATED)
PHILIP D. MOREHEAD, ED.
- First full revision since the original 1958 publication
- More than 20,000 new words and phrases
- 1,500 additional entries
- Synonyms and antonyms for each word listed
- New feature: famous quotes and phrases

THE NEW AMERICAN WEBSTER HANDY COLLEGE DICTIONARY (4TH EDITION)
PHILIP D. MOREHEAD, ED.
The essential dictionary for every school, college, office, and home. Inside this bestseller you'll find more features than in any other pocket dictionary.

SIGNET

BOOKS THAT CHANGED THE WORLD

BY ROBERT B. DOWNS

This lucidly organized collection distills the key ideas of the works that have had the most influence on Western history and culture, from the Bible to the *Iliad*, the *Republic* and *The Prince* to *Civil Disobedience*, *Das Kapital*, *The Interpretation of Dreams*, and *Silent Spring*, this is an essential guide to Western thought.